S0-DNL-568

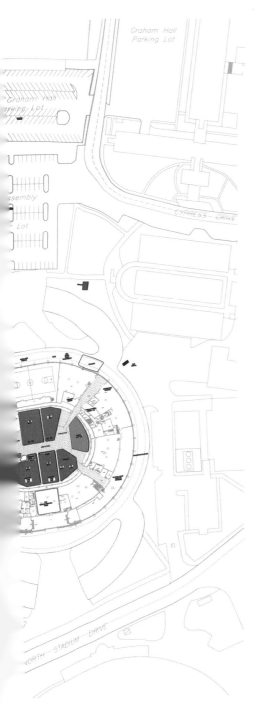

INDEX

LSU *in the* Eye *of the* Storm

LSU in the Eye of the Storm

A UNIVERSITY MODEL FOR DISASTER RESPONSE

Compiled and written by Renée Bacher and Teresa Devlin
with Kristine Calongne, Joshua Duplechain, and
Stephanie Pertuit

With a Foreword by
Sean O'Keefe, Chancellor of Louisiana State University

Photo editor: Jim Zietz
Designer: Laura Gleason

NOVEMBER 2005

This book is dedicated to the thousands of humanitarians at LSU, throughout Louisiana, across the United States, and around the world who helped in our greatest time of need.

The only nation is humanity.

—Author unknown

FOREWORD

When I became chancellor of Louisiana State University, the state's largest public university, I was charged with the responsibility of a city within a city. Indeed, the university carries out many of the same operations as the capital city of Baton Rouge, in which it resides. Equipped with its own police force, public affairs office, Reserve Officer Training Corps, facility and dining services, maintenance and grounds crews, athletic facilities, and many other facilities and operations, LSU has a wide array of resources. And all of these resources were needed in order to meet LSU's responsibilities in the wake of the devastating Hurricane Katrina.

On the morning of August 29, 2005, the worst natural disaster in U.S. history slammed into the Gulf Coast with 145-mph winds. The eye of the storm passed over portions of Plaquemines, St. Bernard, Orleans, and St. Tammany parishes in Louisiana and then over Hancock County, Mississippi. The storm directly affected 90,000 square miles in seven states. The damage to the LSU campus, some 150 miles from the coast of the Gulf of Mexico, was minimal. But just to the southeast, the state's largest city, New Orleans, was inundated by water from Katrina's storm surge, which overwhelmed the levees that protect the city. The rapidly rising water forced thousands of citizens into attics and onto rooftops, where many were trapped for several days in the debilitating heat, awaiting rescue.

Immediately following the storm, LSU recognized a need to help the victims of this tragedy. The university mobilized its resources and put in place a system that allowed evacuees to find refuge on our campus. Before long, LSU found itself squarely in the figurative eye of the storm.

LSU's Carl Maddox Field House operated as a special-needs shelter for residents of nursing homes and other attended-care facilities even before the storm hit land. Immediately after the storm, medical relief efforts expanded into the nearby Pete Maravich Assembly Center. As the situation in New Orleans worsened, the operation evolved into a full-scale medical facility. The surgeon general of the United States observed that LSU had become the largest acute-care hospital established in a contingency in the nation's history. The 800-bed operation triaged more than 15,000 patients in the days following the storm; treated more than 6,000 patients; filled more than 2,000 prescriptions for evacuees; provided food, water, and clothing to the victims; and helped to reunite families that had been separated during the evacuation.

Evacuees were transported the approximately 75 miles from New Orleans to Baton Rouge by bus, helicopter, and ambulance. The helicopters landed at LSU's Bernie Moore Track Stadium. LSU Police, with the help of the National Guard, blocked streets to make way for the emergency vehicles and maintained security at the hospital

LSU chancellor Sean O'Keefe (left) and U.S. surgeon general Richard H. Carmona (right) walk outside the Pete Maravich Assembly Center.

Jim Zietz/LSU Office of Public Affairs

facilities and around the LSU campus. Approximately 3,000 students, faculty, and staff volunteered to work at the hospitals and shelters. Hundreds of doctors and medical professionals from the LSU System and from around the country volunteered to work long hours with no sleep to care for the evacuees.

LSU's Office of Public Affairs along with university volunteers staffed a 24-hour emergency hotline and a separate Emergency Operations Center to provide critical communication and coordinate response efforts. Public Affairs' Media Relations Department and operations staff handled thousands of media calls from around the globe and ushered more than 100 reporters through the hospital facilities on campus. Admissions officers worked around the clock to admit more than 3,000 students who attended universities in the New Orleans area. Experts from LSU's Hurricane Center as well as researchers on campus in other disciplines provided news agencies with information and insight. In short, all hands were on deck and performed heroically.

Looking back, I realized that it was a herculean effort. This book details that effort, day by day, and constructs what we at LSU believe is a model for disaster response by a university. It is my hope that the information provided within, and the lessons that we learned during this crisis, may help those confronted by such a crisis in the future.

Along with teaching and research, part of LSU's mission is also public service. And in this instance, the LSU community took that public service component to a new level. The spirit of cooperation that I witnessed, among not only LSU employees but local, state, and federal agencies was inspiring. The red tape that often slows large government agencies was cut at LSU, and the unspoken motto was "get it done."

Indeed, the incredible group of people at LSU identified and performed tasks so efficiently that jobs that would typically have been burdensome or time-consuming were carried out so smoothly they might almost have gone unnoticed. Fences were put up to provide security around the hospitals, computers and telephone lines were installed in the call center and Emergency Operations Center, food was delivered, patients were cared for, and everything that needed to be done was done.

While we do not claim to have performed every task perfectly, I am incredibly proud of the job that this university did under terrifying and chaotic conditions. It has been said that what does not kill us makes us stronger. I believe that LSU is indeed stronger for having gone through this ordeal. We are stronger in our sense of community, stronger in our knowledge of how to perform during a crisis, stronger in our sense of public service. If the storm clouds of Hurricane Katrina had any silver lining at all, it is the fact that LSU is more unified, more knowledgeable, and better prepared to assist our community as we continue down the long road to recovery.

Sean O'Keefe
LSU Chancellor

LSU *in the* Eye *of the* Storm

1

HURRICANE PREPARATION DAY
SATURDAY, AUGUST 27, 2005

- On August 4, 2005, LSU researchers warned that the 2005 hurricane season could be historic.
- At 5:00 a.m., Katrina was designated a Category 3 hurricane. It was the eleventh named storm and the third major hurricane of 2005.

A CALM CONCERN BEFORE THE STORM

Two days before Hurricane Katrina made landfall in Louisiana, the skies were clear, a humid breeze was blowing, and the telephones started ringing in the Office of Public Affairs at Louisiana State University in Baton Rouge. A handful of callers wanted to know whether classes would be canceled on Monday, the predicted day of the storm.

TRAFFIC BUILDS

Low-lying areas in coastal Louisiana were under mandatory evacuation orders, and the mayor of New Orleans called for a voluntary evacuation. Those leaving were advised to take enough provisions to last three days.

> "Even as we were scurrying around buying gallons of bottled water, in the back of my mind I thought Katrina would be like Hurricane Ivan was for New Orleans: much ado about nothing. If only."
>
> —LSU ART PROFESSOR

Baton Rouge, 75 miles west of New Orleans, was expecting severe weather, but not a direct hit. Lafayette, the closest city to the west of Baton Rouge, is normally an hour away by car and was expected to be further from the path of the storm. But contraflow had already begun on Interstate 10 (meaning all lanes would flow west, away from New Orleans). Traffic was consequently heavy in Baton Rouge, and the trip to Lafayette could take several hours. Some evacuees began to settle in to Baton Rouge to ride out the predicted storm.

SPECIAL-NEEDS SHELTER

Residents of assisted-living facilities and nursing homes were among the first to arrive in Baton Rouge. LSU had a Special Needs Shelter Plan in place; in the event of an evacuation of surrounding areas, this shelter was to provide medically dependent individuals with an appropriate place to stay. Twenty-four hours earlier, the Carl Maddox

Field House, normally the site of championship indoor track meets, had become the site of this shelter. The state Department of Social Services and Department of Health and Hospitals were working 12-hour shifts, caring for those who had arrived and readying the place for its capacity of 250 inhabitants at the height of the predicted disaster. A standby generator had been dispatched from Chicago and was expected to arrive Monday.

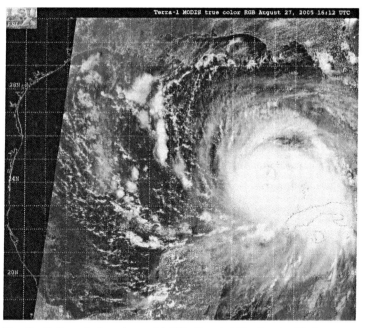

The Earth Scan Laboratory of LSU's Coastal Studies Institute captured this image of Hurricane Katrina from the Terra-1 MODIS satellite.

GETTING THE WORD OUT ON SAFETY

LSU Police met with the chancellor, student affairs personnel, and other campus groups to discuss security preparations for the storm. LSU's Office of Public Affairs issued a press release about what was happening on campus and updated the LSU Web site accordingly. An e-mail broadcast from the chancellor to students, faculty, and staff announced that all classes and public events on campus would be canceled Monday, and all nonessential business at LSU was to be suspended in order to ensure safety on campus and allow people to gather with family and friends at what might prove to be a challenging time. Information would follow about whether school would reopen on Tuesday. Students, faculty, and staff were urged to monitor the LSU Web site and local radio stations for continuous information about the storm. Crisis evacuation centers were identified at three area public schools should students need them.

Through a broadcast e-mail of its own, the Department of Residential Life advised students to take precautions as the storm passed over Baton Rouge. They advised students to stay inside at all times during the storm, stay in hallways and away from windows, reserve telephone calls for emergencies, and keep in mind that everything is calm when the eye of a hurricane passes overhead, so they should not be tricked into stepping outside for a quick look.

PREPARED BUT OPTIMISTIC

In recent years, there had been a handful of monster storms brewing in the Gulf that seemed destined for Louisiana. But none had done catastrophic damage to the most populous part of the state. Despite preparations being made for the arrival of what was today a Category 3 storm, the atmosphere on campus was pensive but not panicked. School was canceled Monday as a routine precaution. If only we'd had an inkling of what was to come.

2

HURRICANE PREPARATION DAY
SUNDAY, AUGUST 28, 2005

- At 12:40 a.m., Hurricane Katrina was designated a Category 4 hurricane. By 7:00 a.m., it reached Category 5 status. A National Weather Service bulletin described the system as having "unprecedented strength."
- At its peak, when the storm was still miles from the coastline, Katrina's maximum sustained winds were measured at 175 mph, with gusts of up to 216 mph.

THE MONSTER HAD GROWN

By morning, Hurricane Katrina had grown into a Category 5 hurricane, and at 9:00 a.m., New Orleans was under its first-ever mandatory evacuation order. A bulletin from the National Weather Service issued at 10:11 a.m. predicted "devastating damage." The Weather Service warned that Katrina was expected to render her target "uninhabitable for weeks . . . perhaps longer."

An anchor from WWL-TV of New Orleans reads over his notes during a break in broadcasting from the Manship School of Mass Communication's television studios in Hodges Hall.

Scott Sternberg/*Daily Reveille*

Even the New Orleans CBS affiliate, WWL-TV, had evacuated and would set up today on campus in Hodges Hall. At LSU's Office of Public Affairs, the telephones began ringing without reprieve. The *New York Times* called. CNN called. LSU students and their parents called. The national media wanted to know where to find accommodations in town and what electronic capabilities the university had. Parents wanted to know where students would be housed in the event that the LSU campus would have to be closed. Was there a designated shelter on campus designed to sustain the 80-mph winds with which Katrina was expected to slam Baton Rouge?

Although Baton Rouge was not under an evacuation order, parents wanted to be sure that students would be safe in their residence halls. Some parents from the evacuated areas wanted to know if they could stay in the residence halls with their children. Everyone essentially wanted to know how LSU would manage and whether the university had a disaster plan.

TRAFFIC IS A NIGHTMARE

Gridlock took hold of Baton Rouge, a city that struggled with traffic flow even under normal circumstances; the drive from New Orleans to Lafayette that could normally be made in about 2 hours could now take up to 15. Travelers intending to pass through Baton Rouge were running out of gas en route to points north and west, and lines at the pump were long. On campus, the chancellor and LSU staff were focused on the logistics of making preparations for an onslaught of people with a variety of needs.

ACADEMIC AFFAIRS EXTENDS DEADLINES

The last day to add classes or to drop courses without receiving withdrawal notices on transcripts would coincide with the arrival of Katrina. Consequently, the Office of Academic Affairs broadcast an e-mail announcing that those deadlines would be extended by as many days as the university would be closed for the hurricane. Special consideration was asked for students who might have to miss additional classes for cleanup after the hurricane, particularly for students in the National Guard.

> "The day before the storm was hectic. . . . I remember thinking I wasn't nearly prepared enough for this thing. The satellite images of Katrina just looked like it was swallowing the Gulf."
>
> —GRADUATE STUDENT

ALL NEWS, ALL THE TIME

One day before the storm made landfall, LSU's telephone recordings and Web site were changed to convey the news that the cancellation of classes had been extended by an additional day, through Tuesday, August 30.

KLSU-FM, LSU's student-operated radio station, in cooperation with the Office of the Chancellor, began providing information and updates to the campus community. LSU was one of the isolated areas in Baton Rouge that did not lose power, and KLSU was one of the few radio stations that operated continuously throughout the storm. Consequently, for those who had no power but did have battery-operated radios, 5,000-watt KLSU became an essential service for disseminating information to the entire city of Baton Rouge and surrounding areas.

3

KATRINA STRIKES

MONDAY, AUGUST 29, 2005

- Hurricane Katrina made landfall near Buras, Louisiana, at 6:10 a.m. with 145-mph winds. By 9:00 a.m., levee breaches flooded New Orleans's lower Ninth Ward with six to eight feet of water. Two hours later St. Bernard Parish, east of the city, was estimated to be under 10 feet of water.

- The LSU Fire and Emergency Training Institute, which has the largest structural-collapse rescue equipment cache in the state, rescued more than 1,800 trapped citizens from their homes in New Orleans.

- An estimated five million homes throughout the Gulf Coast region lost power because of Hurricane Katrina.

AN UNWELCOME GUEST ARRIVES

As Katrina's gusts swept across Baton Rouge, the early-morning skies darkened and the wind began to howl. Hours later, trees that had stood for more than a hundred years were ripped up by their roots across the city, toppling onto houses and across roadways and taking out power lines as they fell. On campus, small crepe myrtle trees, branches, and debris littered the ground, but the majestic live oaks remained standing. Thanks to the campus Cogeneration Facility, the heart of campus had power throughout the storm and in its aftermath, even when the rest of Baton Rouge did not. However, cell phone coverage was sporadic, and the LSU Web site suffered outages that were diagnosed and corrected quickly by the university's Information Technology Services department. As soon as the Web site was up and running, LSU's Office of Public Affairs distributed a release saying faculty and staff would be expected to return to campus on Wednesday, August 31, and classes would resume on Thursday, September 1. The release went on to explain that employees were expected to return to work only if they could do so safely.

> "With new information coming in around the clock, I had to update the LSU Web site from home during and after the storm. One glitch: we had no electricity. So I used a converter to run my laptop off the car battery and ran a 30-foot telephone line out to my vehicle so I could dial in. It was a bit slow, but it got the job done."
>
> —DIRECTOR OF CREATIVE SERVICES, LSU PUBLIC AFFAIRS

Hurricane Katrina's damage to the levee system left 80 percent of New Orleans flooded.

FLOOD WATERS RISE AND LSU STAFF GEAR UP FOR VISITORS

There were reports that the levees in New Orleans had breached early in the morning, but the reports were not confirmed until later in the afternoon. The city had filled with water like a giant soup bowl.

LSU professional staff members spent the night in the Student Recreation Complex so it could be opened as quickly as possible the following day to provide assistance. The Department of Residential Life's administrative building was turned into a residence hall as 15 staff members stayed through the night. Residential Life's education group used a telephone tree to get regular updates on how LSU students were faring in various buildings. During this time, Facility Services staff continued to respond to calls for repairs at residence halls and on-campus apartments.

LSU FIRE AND EMERGENCY TRAINING INSTITUTE DEPLOYED

Meanwhile, in Shreveport, Louisiana, the LSU Fire and Emergency Training Institute (LSU FETI) staff were activated. The search-and-rescue staff had been conducting an 80-hour rescue specialist course when they were instructed to return to Baton Rouge with their equipment and await deployment to New Orleans.

LSU FETI has the largest structural-collapse rescue equipment cache in the state and was able to deploy two 40-foot trailers fully equipped with rescue equipment, including concrete- and metal-cutting devices and specialized shoring mechanisms. Ultimately, nearly 800 firefighters from across Louisiana, the United States, and France would also be deployed by the Federal Emergency Management Agency (FEMA) at the request of the state Office of Homeland Security and Emergency Preparedness to perform rescue work. They brought 200 apparatuses and support vehicles to the city. Despite cell phone outages and other communication issues hampering their efforts, the LSU FETI team would rescue more than 1,800 people from their New Orleans homes.

4

FIRST DAY OUT

TUESDAY, AUGUST 30, 2005

- Approximately 15,000 evacuees were triaged at LSU and subsequently referred to shelters and special-needs facilities.
- Approximately 6,000 patients affected by Katrina were cared for at the field hospital on campus.

PETE MARAVICH ASSEMBLY CENTER OPENS FOR TRIAGE

As citizens of New Orleans were rescued from floodwaters and rooftops, those with serious injuries were taken by ambulance and helicopter to the Pete Maravich Assembly Center (PMAC), ordinarily home to LSU basketball, volleyball, and gymnastics. The PMAC would serve as a triage center. From there, the seriously ill and injured were transported to Baton Rouge hospitals. But soon local hospitals were at capacity, and the PMAC and the Carl Maddox Field House combined became a field hospital with 800 beds. The field hospital was later identified as the largest acute-care hospital to date in U.S. history.

As it became clear that the field hospital needed doctors, nurses, and volunteers, the entire LSU community mobilized to find medical personnel, clothing, and supplies. The site, complete with a helipad on neighboring Bernie Moore Track Stadium, would have nearly 3,000 LSU students, staff, and community members working as volunteers on various tasks during the first week after the storm. Many patients at the field hospital were in shock, disoriented, or hysterical. Some volunteers grew emotionally exhausted.

> **"On the way back to the PMAC it looked like a scene from the movie *Outbreak*. . . . Stretchers rolled in constantly, and for the first time in my life, I saw someone die right in front of me."**
>
> **—ATHLETIC DEPARTMENT STUDENT WORKER**

STUDENT MEDIA, UNINTERRUPTED

In the immediate aftermath of the storm, three student disc jockeys and two advisers operated KLSU for 72 hours, uninterrupted. The Office of Student Media and the Manship School of Mass Communication provided displaced New Orleans television (WWL-TV) and print media *(Times-Picayune)* professionals with assistance, space, and support.

The medical evacuation effort at LSU's Pete Maravich Assembly Center following Hurricane Katrina represented the largest deployment of public health officials in U.S. history.

Jim Zietz/LSU Office of Public Affairs

RESIDENTIAL LIFE ACCOMMODATES RECORD NUMBERS

Following the storm, Residential Life was called to provide temporary housing to more than 450 public safety workers as well as displaced University of New Orleans students and families. The job of the day was to quickly identify vacant apartment space on campus and reopen closed buildings. By placing as many as eight beds (four sets of bunk beds) in some on-campus apartments, Residential Life was able to house substantially more people than anyone originally imagined could be accommodated. With the exception of the University of New Orleans students, they allowed each group to sort out its own arrangements for male and female living spaces. Organizations accommodated included FEMA, WWL-TV, and the state departments of Social Services and Wildlife and Fisheries.

CLASS CANCELLATION EXTENDS

In a press release issued August 30, university officials extended the cancellation of classes through September 6. The release added, "all university faculty, staff and administrators should please return to campus to help meet current, emergent evacuation assistance demands, and to begin preparing for the resumption of class next week. . . . The LSU administration has requested that university faculty be understanding and flexible when dealing with the collection of assigned materials and student absences due to the disruption caused by Hurricane Katrina."

5

SECOND DAY OUT

WEDNESDAY, AUGUST 31, 2005

- The LSU Hurricane Information Center's hotline was open for 13 days and answered 6,495 calls.
- The population of the temporary animal shelter set up on campus peaked at 1,287 pets of evacuees.

TIME TO MOVE FORWARD

With Baton Rouge struggling to regain power and much of southeast Louisiana reeling from flooding and destruction, a small amount of normalcy returned to campus. Faculty and nonessential staff reported to work for the first time since Katrina had hit. But work was far from "business as usual."

The hurricane recovery effort continued as the special-needs shelter on campus entered its fifth day of operation and the field hospital embarked on its second day. Campus traffic that ordinarily consisted of students and faculty bustling to and from class now included ambulances, military vehicles, and helicopters. Several roads on campus were restricted to allow emergency-response vehicles direct routes to the field hospital.

Campus teemed with evacuated citizens, emergency relief personnel, and media as well as the numerous guests and families making the most of makeshift accommodations in LSU's residence halls. Faculty and staff were returning to a familiar place, which at first glance bore little evidence that a storm had raged here only days before. But a closer look revealed numerous unfamiliar faces with an expression of tragedy in their eyes.

> **"Even though I have only had five hours of sleep in the past two days, I have no regrets."**
>
> **—LSU INTERIOR DESIGN STUDENT AND FIELD HOSPITAL VOLUNTEER**

A DELUGE OF QUESTIONS

At noon, LSU's Office of Public Affairs opened the LSU Hurricane Information Center, a 24-hour hotline manned by more than 70 LSU faculty, staff, and student volunteers working 8-hour shifts. Each operator had access to the Internet (many callers had no Internet access) and to continuously updated information on campus, local, regional, and national relief efforts.

Operators answered calls from around the country on every imaginable issue, including a few no one expected. Students—from both LSU and the affected areas—requested information on the admissions and resignation processes, university policies, housing, financial aid, and more. Families called desperately searching for loved ones. Those looking for relatives evacuated from New Orleans, southeast Louisiana, Mississippi, and Alabama were directed to national databases. Those looking for relatives attending LSU were directed to the Office of the University Registrar.

Some individuals and organizations called to offer their time and talents as volunteers. Owners searched for details on pet shelters, hoping their animal friends left behind were safe and dry. Students' parents were concerned about the safety of their sons and daughters on campus. Media agencies sought access and information. And countless callers wanted to report, confirm, deny, or dispel the rapidly growing number of rumors regarding crime, flooding, health scares, gas shortages, and more.

DISSEMINATING INFORMATION

While not necessarily equipped to answer each specific question, operators provided callers with information, telephone numbers, and Web addresses. Many in the region remained without power or Internet access, and the call center's operators were also available to search online resources at callers' requests. Above all, operators offered callers empathetic ears.

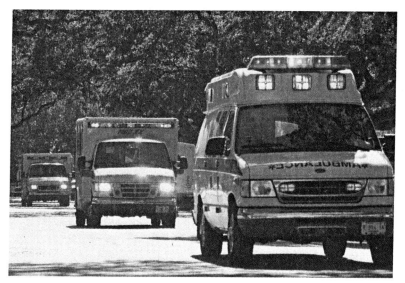

North Stadium Road on LSU's campus was designated an ambulance corridor during the medical evacuation efforts.

Jim Zietz/LSU Office of Public Affairs

The local and toll-free numbers for the LSU hotline were posted on the LSU home page (www.lsu.edu), which had been transformed into a message-board format. Links to press releases, local and national agencies, and other resources were added to the site regularly.

HELP IS ON THE WAY

Volunteers were needed in a variety of capacities, and the response from the campus, local, and national communities was immediate. However, without organization the eagerness of those offering help might interfere with the relief effort as a whole.   .

LSU Student Government, in association with the university's Public Policy Research Laboratory (a joint initiative of the Manship School of Mass Communication and the E. J. Ourso College of Business), created LSU Volunteers, a telephone number and Web site where interested parties—predominantly from the LSU community—could register. The organization then assigned registered volunteers to specific times and tasks. More than 2,500 volunteers nationwide heeded the call. After the immediate need for volunteers was satisfied, the database was maintained to provide continued support to meet needs that would arise in the coming months.

The Louisiana Department of Health and Hospitals (DHH) issued an e-mail seeking "experienced medical professionals, such as doctors and nurses, to assist in Louisiana's recovery effort following Hurricane Katrina." Licensed medical professionals were asked to contact DHH's volunteer line to determine when and where their skills would be needed. Medical volunteers were also encouraged to provide some of their own supplies, including stethoscopes and blood pressure cuffs.

The Office of the Governor announced the launch of

211, another volunteer registry hotline. The three-digit telephone number was not recognized initially by several cellular providers or by the campus telephone network, but Baton Rouge land lines were able to connect volunteers to the database.

UNIVERSITY BUSINESS

Two schools in the LSU System were located in New Orleans: the University of New Orleans (UNO) and the LSU Health Sciences Center (LSUHSC). To better serve their students and employees, both institutions opened satellite offices on LSU's Baton Rouge campus. LSUHSC, which manages New Orleans's Charity Hospital, also established its own 24-hour hotline and temporarily relocated to LSU's Pennington Biomedical Research Center in Baton Rouge.

Classes for all southeast Louisiana schools continued to be suspended, yet thousands of college students, from both LSU and affected schools in New Orleans, were beginning to take stock of the uncertain future ahead of them. While their families confronted the idea of relocating, some students were faced with deciding whether it made sense to resume their studies for the fall semester. Other students, who had enrolled in New Orleans schools from out of state, had to determine the best place to continue. Their residences, their belongings, and in many cases, their automobiles were inaccessible in New Orleans. Was it time to head home? To continue in Louisiana? Or to start over somewhere new? The questions were overwhelming.

To assist students, staff from the Mental Health Service of LSU's Student Health Center made themselves available to those in need, regardless of whether they attended LSU. Within the first few days after the hurricane nearly 100 LSU students opted to resign for the semester. Some had lost loved ones and homes in the hurricane-ravaged parishes; others were facing financial destitution. For thousands of students attending school in New Orleans, returning to school as soon as possible was the next step toward a much-needed routine and a step away from devastation.

LSU's Office of Undergraduate Admissions, the LSU Graduate School, and supporting offices began answering thousands of students' questions about the admissions process, housing, financial aid, and transfers. In responding to these inquiries, LSU administrators strove to accommodate and serve students, employees, and their families to the best of their ability, cutting much of the red tape that can sometimes bog down a university as large as LSU.

THE INFLUX OF MEDIA

More than 100 media representatives visited campus during the two weeks following Hurricane Katrina. LSU hosted journalists from *Good Morning America*, the *Washington Post*, MTV, ESPN, *People* magazine, the *Today Show*, *Dateline NBC*, *Fox NFL Sunday*, the *Village Voice*, the *News Hour with Jim Lehrer*, CNN.com, the *Chronicle of Higher Education*, and several other news media. And many reporters who did not visit the campus called. Celebrities showed their support for the evacuees by visiting the affected areas. Visitors to Louisiana and the LSU area included country music singer and Louisiana native Tim McGraw; actors John Travolta, Kelly Preston, Sean Penn, Will Smith, and Kirstie Alley; and NFL quarterbacks and New Orleans natives Peyton and Eli Manning, among others.

The Office of Public Affairs' Media Relations Department—a team of five full-time employees—set out to accommodate the media without compromising the relief effort or interrupting campus business. The Media Relations team gave tours to members of the press from Japan, Sweden, South Korea, Great Britain, France, and Germany. University faculty shared their expertise with the media on a variety of hurricane-related topics, including hurricane research, disaster management, wind engineering, coastal science, geography, economic impacts, agricultural impacts, evacuation procedures, geology, oceanography, stress management, and more. At times, Media Relations staff had to limit access to some experts who were physically and emotionally affected by the devastation of the hurricane and the high volume of requests.

ASSISTING ANIMAL RESCUE EFFORTS

With pets prohibited at Red Cross shelters, the LSU School of Veterinary Medicine in collaboration with the LSU Agricultural Center, Louisiana Veterinary Medical Association, Louisiana Department of Agriculture and Forestry, Louisiana Society for the Prevention of Cruelty to Animals, and the Louisiana Animal Control Association opened a temporary animal shelter on campus at the LSU Agricultural Center's John M. Parker Agricultural Coliseum. The shelter opened August 31 and within 48 hours took in more than 500 animals. Dogs and cats comprised the overwhelming majority of the population, but the shelter also accepted exotic birds, ducks, chickens, ferrets, mice, gerbils, guinea pigs, tortoises, and a pig.

The shelter was established for animals brought by their owners or veterinarians. The School of Veterinary Medicine managed animal care while the LSU Agricultural Center managed the facility. Built for livestock shows, Parker Coliseum's large animal facilities were modified to support smaller pets. In addition, the Agricultural Center canceled or postponed several events to keep the shelter in place.

Administrators of the animal shelter met daily to discuss

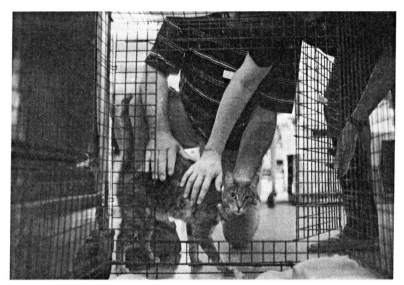

One of the hundreds of New Orleans–area felines sent to the on-campus animal shelter receives a friendly pet from volunteers. The shelter at John M. Parker Coliseum helped to reunite more than 2,000 evacuated pets with their owners.

Jim Zietz/LSU Office of Public Affairs

logistics, such as how to make the best use of volunteers and maintain a sanitary and safe environment for both humans and animals. As pets arrived, they went through an intake process, which included gathering information on the owners and the pets and photographing the pets. Animals were then assigned to specific cage numbers, and the information was added to a database that tracked where each animal was located.

Volunteers from the local community as well as veterinarians, veterinary technicians, students, and other animal-care professionals offered to help staff the on-campus animal shelter.

Jim Zietz/LSU Office of Public Affairs

The School of Veterinary Medicine provided primary and advanced medical and surgical care for the LSU shelter and advanced care for the Humane Society shelter 20 miles east in Gonzales, Louisiana. The veterinary school's intensive care unit more than doubled and was staffed 24 hours a day by LSU faculty and staff and by volunteer veterinarians and technicians from as far away as New York and California. Veterinary school staff used the Internet to keep pet owners, the public, faculty, staff, and students posted on the shelter's progress.

When possible, owners were encouraged to return to the shelter as often as they could to feed, walk, and water their pets, though it was mainly the shelter's hundreds of volunteers who saw to these tasks. Volunteers also cleaned cages, sorted supplies, and gave stressed animals some much-needed attention. Veterinarians, veterinary technicians, and animal control professionals came from across the country and Canada. Baton Rouge and New Orleans–area veterinary professionals also volunteered, along with faculty, staff, and students from the LSU School of Veterinary Medicine. Some faculty were assigned to the shelter and relieved of their regular duties. In addition, an educational block was created for fourth-year veterinary students so that they could receive school credit for working at the shelter.

LSU and the School of Veterinary Medicine played an enormous role in what was the largest pet rescue in U.S. history. Approximately 2,300 dogs, cats, birds, and other animals eventually passed through the LSU shelter, and more than 2,000 pets were eventually reunited with their families. After all the animals had been reunited with their owners or placed in foster care, the shelter closed on October 15.

The importance of pets in today's society is evident by

the number of people who refused to evacuate rather than abandon their pets. In fact, the Katrina experience may have changed the way federal agencies evacuate citizens. When Hurricane Rita hit three weeks after Katrina, some shelters were allowing people to bring their pets.

BACK, BUT NOT BACK TO NORMAL

Many LSU employees came to work seeking a reprieve from the stresses at home—adjusting to life without power, housing evacuated family members, struggling with overtaxed telephone services, searching for hard-to-find gasoline or groceries, assessing the situation of their state. While some expressed feelings of survivor guilt, others faced property damage of their own, although most of the damage paled in comparison to the images and stories making headlines.

Coming to work introduced faculty and staff to a new array of challenges, yet this simple act also provided many with opportunities to work toward solutions, to move forward, and to help others do the same.

Crowds formed long lines to enter the Louisiana Superdome, which opened Saturday, August 27, as a last-resort refuge.

Ted Jackson/*Times-Picayune*

A man clings to a column on his porch as he waits for rescue in the lower Ninth Ward in New Orleans.

Alex Brandon/*Times-Picayune*

Five days after Katrina hit, flooding pervaded St. Bernard Parish.

Ellis Lucia/*Times-Picayune*

The Georgia National Guard rescues a woman from the roof of a two-story house on Tulane Avenue in New Orleans.

Kathy Anderson/*Times-Picayune*

New Orleans Police Department SWAT officers help Ninth Ward residents out of their water-filled home into a waiting boat.

Alex Brandon/*Times-Picayune*

Two military helicopters take off from LSU's Bernie Moore Track Stadium after transporting victims of Hurricane Katrina to the field hospital on campus.

Steve Franz/LSU Sports Information

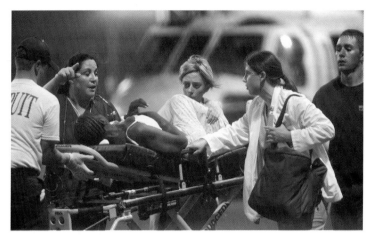

Volunteer medics transfer a New Orleans evacuee from a naval helicopter into the triage center at the Pete Maravich Assembly Center.

Anson Trahan/*Daily Reveille*

A medical volunteer treats a PMAC field hospital patient's needs. In many instances, medical staff served multiple roles, such as doctor, nurse, and counselor.

Jolie Duhon/*Daily Reveille*

Members of the Louisiana National Guard assisted in the efforts of the medical staff and disaster management agencies at the special-needs shelter at LSU's Carl Maddox Field House.

Jim Zietz/LSU Office of Public Affairs

Volunteers provide hurricane victims with supplies at the special-needs shelter in the LSU Field House.

Jim Zietz/LSU Office of Public Affairs

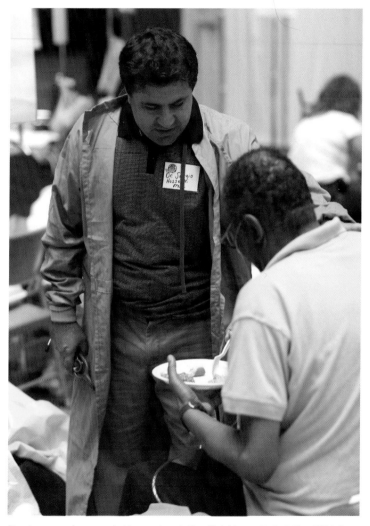

Doctors made rounds throughout the field hospital at the PMAC during their rotations.

Jim Zietz/LSU Office of Public Affairs

The 800-bed medical facility at LSU was said to be the largest acute-care field hospital ever created in U.S. history.

Jim Zietz/LSU Office of Public Affairs

In the LSU Field House, LSU Dining Services provided food and drink to thousands of workers and evacuees during their stay on the LSU campus.

Evacuees filled the Baton Rouge River Center, which became one of many shelters to open west of New Orleans following Katrina.

Chris Perkins/*Daily Reveille*

LSU students Autumn Crosset (center) and Jay Moore (right) deliver supplies to Hurricane Katrina victims sheltered at the Baton Rouge River Center.

Chris Perkins/*Daily Reveille*

Participating in the largest pet rescue in U.S. history, the LSU School of Veterinary Medicine cared for more than 2,000 pets in a temporary animal shelter in LSU's Parker Coliseum.

Jim Zietz/LSU Office of Public Affairs

The LSU School of Veterinary Medicine and the LSU Agricultural Center joined efforts to transform John M. Parker Coliseum, usually used for livestock shows, into a temporary animal shelter for 46 days.

Jim Zietz/LSU Office of Public Affairs

In a week's time, volunteers at LSU's Hurricane Information Center received more than 6,000 calls from students, parents, and citizens across the country.

Jim Zietz/LSU Office of Public Affairs

On September 2, LSU chancellor Sean O'Keefe discussed the university's relief efforts at a town hall meeting for the campus community.

Jim Zietz/LSU Office of Public Affairs

An American Red Cross representative expresses his gratitude to those who joined the relief effort during the town hall meeting at LSU's Campbell Auditorium.

At a press conference and tour on September 4, U.S. secretary of Health and Human Services Michael Leavitt introduces Chris Trevino, M.D., medical director of the field hospital at the LSU Field House and Pete Maravich Assembly Center.

Jim Zietz/LSU Office of Public Affairs

Trevino, Leavitt, U.S. surgeon general Richard H. Carmona, and Centers for Disease Control and Prevention director Julie Gerberding meet with personnel of the medical facility in the PMAC.

Jim Zietz/LSU Office of Public Affairs

A *National Geographic* film crew interviews Associate Professor Ivor van Heerden, deputy director of the LSU Hurricane Center and director of the LSU Center for the Study of Public Health Impacts of Hurricanes, at the London Avenue canal breach in New Orleans.

As students returned to class, campus streets were lined with military vehicles, such as these parked behind the Journalism Building.

In tribute to Katrina victims, LSU football players' helmets were embellished for 2005 with the Louisiana state flag, an image of the states affected by the hurricane, and the fleur-de-lis, traditional symbol of Louisiana and New Orleans.

6

THIRD DAY OUT

THURSDAY, SEPTEMBER 1, 2005

- Prior to Hurricane Katrina, 10 college campuses were based in New Orleans.
- Combined, the institutions in New Orleans enrolled more than 67,000 students.

AN EDUCATION IN DESTRUCTION

An article published in the September 16, 2005, issue of the *Chronicle of Higher Education* reported 31 institutions were in areas affected by Katrina. Ten of those were in New Orleans: Delgado Community College, Dillard University, the LSU Health Sciences Center (LSUHSC), Loyola University New Orleans, New Orleans Baptist Theological Seminary, Our Lady of Holy Cross College, Southern University at New Orleans, Tulane University, the University of New Orleans (UNO), and Xavier University of Louisiana. Collectively, these institutions enrolled more than 67,000 students.

Immediately following the storm, all campuses suspended classes. Some planned to reopen by midsemester, at other locations in most cases. Others, including Dillard, Loyola, Tulane, and Xavier, announced they would be closed for the semester.

THE POPULATION CONTINUES TO GROW

> "A student from an affected institution noted that we had succeeded in registering more students in 10 days than all of the students enrolled at his school. During the normal admissions process, it takes us [LSU] about a year to admit and register approximately 5,000 new students. We did 60 percent of that number in 10 days."
>
> **—VICE PROVOST FOR ACADEMIC AFFAIRS**

To help displaced students, LSU, like many schools nationwide and a handful of international schools, expedited the admissions process and waived application and late fees. The Office of Undergraduate Admissions extended the original post-hurricane application deadline by one week. A one-stop operation was established so that new students could complete the application, registration, and orientation processes in one location. This effort required the cooperation of a multitude of offices on campus, including the Office of Undergraduate Admissions, the Office of the University Registrar, the Office of Bursar Operations, the Office of Student Aid and Scholarships, the Office of Recruiting Services, Orientation,

Theresa Mooney (right), a counselor from LSU's College of Art and Design, assists one of the more than 2,800 displaced students who enrolled at LSU after Katrina. A one-stop registration center was established to expedite the application, registration, and orientation processes.

Prather Warren/LSU Office of Public Affairs

the Department of Residential Life, and faculty and counselors from all academic colleges. The registration center was open from Thursday, September 1, through noon on Monday, September 12, including the Saturday and Monday of the Labor Day weekend.

During this time, 237 faculty and staff helped to admit 3,285 students and register approximately 2,800 for the fall semester. Deans and department chairs had to continually monitor enrollment in courses, expand section sizes, and locate new instructors to accommodate the student population, which had increased by more than 10 percent. Eighty new class sections were made available as well.

Crowd control was necessary to maintain an orderly flow in a congested area in hot weather. Displaced students and staff working the registration center showed remarkable flexibility and patience under trying conditions.

THE ON-CAMPUS REAL ESTATE BOOM

College students displaced by Katrina needed not only a new school but housing and transportation, as many had lost their vehicles. Prior to the hurricane, LSU's 19 residence halls and 2 on-campus apartment complexes were near capacity. In the days following the hurricane, two residence facilities that had been closed were made available. More than 450 beds were made available to organizations such as relief workers, state and federal agencies, volunteer medical staff, and media professionals from the New Orleans area.

More than 350 family members of students living on campus had evacuated to those students' residence halls and campus apartments. While the Department of Residential Life never advertised this service, housing staff did not turn families away. In the days following the hurricane, Residential Life actively sought alternate housing for displaced family members staying with student residents by using an on-campus database as well as shareyourhome.org, a citywide database created to help evacuated citizens find temporary housing in the community. Residential Life also alleviated some stress for students and their families by hosting Family Fun Day, which provided food, games, tours of campus, counseling, and massage therapy to participants.

By asking residents with private rooms to volunteer to accept one roommate each, adding accommodations for one more to larger rooms, and converting some lounges into rooms, the Department of Residential Life processed and housed nearly 500 new assignments, while continuing to house relief workers and New Orleans–area professionals. Approximately 300 more displaced students were added to a waiting list. As an added service, Residential Life staff established a list of Baton Rouge citizens willing to host displaced students. The staff allowed students and host families to match themselves by providing interested parties with the appropriate contact information.

Throughout the hurricane response efforts, hall staff organized activities and events for residents. These included movie nights; athletics; board games; Ping Pong, pool, and video game tournaments; and painting. As unreliable

Noelle Moreau, a doctoral student in kinesiology and a physical thera-pist in Baton Rouge, provides supplies to a member of the National Guard in the PMAC field hospital.

Jim Zietz/LSU Office of Public Affairs

cellular service made it difficult for students to communi-cate with their families, the department increased the num-ber of telephones available in the lobbies of several halls.

VOLUNTEERS STILL NEEDED

On the second day back, volunteers were still needed for a variety of efforts. LSU students and employees proved to be a ready and willing force, quickly responding to an e-mail from the chancellor and LSU System president. Members of the campus community who wanted to help were asked to register with LSU Volunteers by telephone or online so that they could be properly managed and dispatched. The e-mail also conveyed the need to provide "short-term and longer-term housing" to students, faculty, and staff from the University of New Orleans and the LSU Health Sciences Center.

Volunteers were needed to assist with meeting needs of evacuated citizens; supporting the efforts of local, state, and federal relief agencies; providing necessary resources and facilities to carry out response efforts; and addressing the needs of our own campus community. The people of LSU's departments and programs filled these needs with creative thinking.

University Recreation, the department overseeing the campus's 112,000-square-foot recreational center, provided housing, activities, space and resources, laundry services, shower services, personal items, and refreshments. The center housed more than 500 relief workers from agencies including Louisiana's Department of Social Services; the federal Drug Enforcement Administration; the state Department of Wildlife and Fisheries; FEMA's Veterinary Medical Assistance Team, Disaster Management Assistance Team, and Disaster Mortuary Operational Response Team; the

FBI; and others. University Recreation also provided computer access, telephone access with conference call capabilities, meeting space, toiletries, towels, fresh linens, fresh shirts and laundry assistance, a meditation/quiet room, and a lounge with refreshments and a television. The center's showers were made available to more than 1,000 volunteers and relief workers.

University Recreation staff provided children's programming to some of the youth in the campus field hospital and special-needs shelter. The recreation center's $7 guest fees were suspended from August 30 through September 6 so that students, faculty, and staff could bring families to the facility. Staff also relocated some regular activities such as aerobics classes to residence halls in order to provide these services to students without disrupting the relief efforts.

The LSU Union provided housing, food, activities, and resources such as e-mail stations during this time. The LSU Child Care Center provided for 25 displaced families; collected, sorted, and distributed supplies; and provided free babysitting to visiting student parents. Career Services offered programs to assist anyone who had lost a job as a result of the hurricane. The Center for Academic Success, the College of Education, and the Cain Center for Scientific, Technological, Engineering, and Mathematical Literacy responded to East Baton Rouge Parish's needs for accommodating new elementary through high school students. Programs were also created to help students transferring to LSU learn their way around campus, identify resources, and understand the university's online services.

The eight-person staff of the Mental Health Service (MHS) trained counselors from LSU's academic units and Career Services so that they could better assist students, employees, and evacuated citizens. MHS staff also extended services to employees of UNO, the medical staff of LSUHSC's Charity Hospital, and journalists and technical staff from New Orleans television station WWL, which was operating on campus. Many of these individuals lost their homes in the flooding and had no housing, transportation, or cash. The demand of their positions and the extent of their loss left them battling waves of depression between alternating rushes of adrenaline. Counselors from MHS were critical in helping them to deal with these issues.

E-MAIL ON SAFETY CONCERNS

With Katrina's aftermath dominating local and national media, information overload was becoming evident on campus. Replayed images of looting in New Orleans saturated the airwaves and caused some concern that an increase in crime and civil unrest had come to Baton Rouge. Rumors began to fly that downtown Baton Rouge, host to a Red

Cross shelter with more than 5,000 evacuees, had experienced increased crime, carjackings, and a riot. Students, parents, and local citizens contacted LSU to report rumors and seek guidance.

In response, the chancellor issued a broadcast e-mail to all members of the campus community, which stated in part:

> There have been confirmed reports of civil unrest in the Baton Rouge area this morning. These incidents appear to be confined to specific areas in the downtown Baton Rouge area and specific locations around the community. At this time, local law enforcement are reported to have the situation contained. To ensure safety, we have instructed that all buildings on campus be locked and we ask that occupants remain indoors.

The e-mail continued to express confidence in the "security procedures of LSU Public Safety" and explained that the additional precaution of locked doors would "permit their timely response to any incidents that may occur on our campus."

7

FOURTH DAY OUT

FRIDAY, SEPTEMBER 2, 2005

- LSU athletic equipment staff laundered 4,000 pounds of bed linens and clothing for Hurricane Katrina survivors housed on campus.
- LSU athletes, coaches, and their spouses spent countless hours folding clean laundry.

MORE HELP ON THE WAY

To assist the relief efforts in Baton Rouge, the Arkansas Department of Health and Human Services dispatched a two-person team that specialized in public health and crisis communications. The Arkansas team assisted LSU's Office of Public Affairs media management efforts and worked with the Louisiana Department of Health and Hospitals officials in the Joint Information Center of the state's Emergency Operations Center.

To stay informed about which news agencies were on campus and to monitor media access in restricted areas, the

Office of Public Affairs established a media credentialing post at its office on the eastern edge of campus. After submitting their names, contact information (including e-mail and cell phone numbers), and affiliations, news crews received media badges, maps of campus, notes about Baton Rouge and resources located near campus, as well as access to media briefings and guided tours.

INCREASING TECHNOLOGICAL SUPPORT

On campus, Information Technology Services (ITS) continued to support relief efforts by tailoring technology—from telephones to Web sites, security access to databases—for the needs at hand. ITS built a message board for the LSU community to list and exchange resources, assisted in the registration of students, provided LSU e-mail accounts to incoming students, and facilitated donations and vendor contacts.

ITS also extended services to the University of New Orleans (UNO) and the LSU Health Sciences Center (LSUHSC). After the storm, UNO officials created a temporary Web site to communicate with students, employees, and supporters. With the help of ITS, UNO's original Web site returned online on Friday. The ITS training center was converted into facilities for UNO's information technology office, and UNO Web, e-mail, and other mission-critical applications were being restored by UNO personnel in the ITS facilities at LSU. ITS also created special emergency information systems applications to serve the payroll and accounting needs of UNO and LSUHSC. The security of a paycheck alleviated anxieties of some of these institutions' employees.

TOWN HALL MEETING

To continue communication efforts and to foster two-way communication, the chancellor led a town hall meeting. While sirens wailed outside and helicopters could be heard overhead, all members of the campus community—including anyone brought to LSU by Katrina—were invited to the approximately 90-minute session in a 1,100-seat auditorium near the heart of campus. (ITS also broadcast the assembly live online and made recordings available on the Web.)

The chancellor opened the forum by addressing the audience, likening the situation to "9/11 in slow motion." He updated the audience on the state of the campus and reminded everyone that the upcoming semester would be unlike any before. Flexibility would be paramount, and the university would do whatever it could to keep daily operations running as smoothly as possible. He praised students for their efforts, flexibility, and willingness to help and welcome their neighbors.

At the town hall meeting on September 2, Monica Clark, student body president of the University of New Orleans, thanked the LSU community for its support.

Jim Zietz/LSU Office of Public Affairs

The audience posed questions to the chancellor and offered comments to the community. Student volunteers encouraged more volunteers. A representative from the Red Cross was moved to tears as he expressed his appreciation for the community so willing to help in such a dire situation. When asked to comment on the previous day's e-mail regarding civil unrest, the chancellor apologized, calling it an overstatement; campus safety had been his first concern.

8

FIFTH DAY OUT

SATURDAY, SEPTEMBER 3, 2005

- During the three-week period of Hurricane Katrina relief efforts, the LSU Web site received more than 2.5 million page views.

- More than 50 of LSU's faculty and staff were interviewed by the media as experts on topics related to Hurricane Katrina, generating hundreds of radio, television, and Internet news stories.

STREAMLINING COMMUNICATIONS

As the days progressed, LSU would have to facilitate communications between campus relief operations and state officials to ensure the most complete care possible for all individuals affected by Katrina. It was the responsibility of LSU personnel to devise methods for all parties involved to communicate effectively.

In response to this need, LSU established the Emergency Operations Center (EOC) to provide information and support for medical personnel and to serve as a conduit for information between LSU and state officials. The university released a broadcast e-mail announcing the creation of the center, stating that the EOC would serve as the single point of contact for organizing resources and communications already established on the LSU campus, better enabling LSU to coordinate its public safety, public affairs, facility services, and other resources in support of the medical relief effort.

> "On one of my daily visits to the field hospital to assess what was needed, patients and medical workers asked me repeatedly for *Community Coffee,* a local brand favored by Louisianians. I put out the word, and within the day, 50 bags appeared."
>
> **—VOLUNTEER**

The EOC was staffed by members of the National Center for Biomedical Research and Training (NCBRT), an organization on campus involved in research, curricula development, training, and other activities pertaining to the possible effects of weapons of mass destruction. NCBRT's specialization in this area made the organization particularly valuable to disaster response and recovery efforts.

Two daily briefings were conducted by the chancellor, EOC staff, state officials, national officials, and representatives of campus relief operations. The briefings covered all aspects of the relief efforts on the LSU campus and in the surrounding community. The EOC remained open 24 hours a day, every day, for more than two weeks. Though the EOC was designed primarily to coordinate communications between the university and state officials, a representative of the Office of Public Affairs was on staff at the EOC to field questions from the media and the public. Public Affairs also sent representatives to the state Office of Homeland Security and Emergency Preparedness to gather and disseminate information.

CHANCELLOR'S CALL FOR DONATIONS

In response to countless calls from individuals wanting to help, a donation point was established at a gymnasium not far from the field hospital. The site was created to aid displaced families of students, faculty, and staff. As word spread about the drop-off site, the influx of donations was staggering. Within one day, the gymnasium was brimming with supplies. During the next six days, more than 150 volunteers helped to collect, sort, and distribute bags of donated clothing. The donations from this site also served to restock both the special-needs shelter and the field hospital with supplies such as toiletries, clothing, and shoes. Displaced students and family members, as well as other displaced families now in the community, were invited to take whatever they needed.

Supplies were stacked at the triage center inside Alex Box Stadium, LSU's baseball venue. As buses arrived, those evacuating were given access to food, water, and restrooms. Medical personnel then evaluated each individual to determine the next step.

Jim Zietz/LSU Office of Public Affairs

MANAGING THE MEDIA

In an effort to restrict the number of media personnel in the field hospital, the Office of Public Affairs initially instituted a plan to pool media. However, because of media demand, as well as the desire of LSU to provide equal access, Public Affairs gave guided tours to all media. These tours gave all credentialed media representatives limited access to the facilities. Media were allowed to take photographs, provided

The animal shelter received truckloads of supplies, ranging from food to cat litter. Items were inventoried and stored on site at Parker Coliseum. Remaining supplies were donated to other shelters.

the images preserved patients' rights to privacy. LSU officials designated two media coordinators as the only individuals authorized to lead the tours through the field hospital.

Having developed a method for providing tours of the facilities, the Office of Public Affairs designated a staging area where the media could meet the coordinators, thus streamlining the process of touring the field hospital. To provide media outlets with stills and footage that LSU personnel had gathered, Public Affairs created CDs and VHS tapes that were made available on request and at the media credentialing area. These stills and footage encompassed many emotionally moving recovery activities at LSU.

During this time period, the five-member Media Relations team was stretched to the limit and needed help. Communication coordinators from several departments on campus volunteered. Staff members also called upon family and friends to serve as support staff, including one employee's mother-in-law who spent hours applying iron-on letters to create "Media Coordinator" T-shirts to identify staff members.

THE MISSING AND THE DEAD

In the rush to escape a deluged New Orleans, many family members became separated. To help reconnect missing friends and relatives on campus, LSU's Information Technology Services worked with Microsoft representatives to create a patient registry, which would provide happy reunions for some.

As with any hospital, a mortuary was a necessary part of the field hospital on campus. A temporary morgue was created to accommodate this inevitable need, a step previously unimaginable for the college campus. LSU and medical staff followed guidelines established by the Pan American Health Organization, a subsidiary of the World Health Organization. The guidelines specified proper handling of the dead, mandated the exhaustion of all attempts to identify the deceased, and dispelled notions that victims of natural disasters posed threats of spreading infection. Only a fraction of Katrina's casualties would pass through LSU before reaching their final resting places, but these guidelines offered direction on how to treat these individuals with respect and dignity.

9

SIXTH DAY OUT
SUNDAY, SEPTEMBER 4, 2005

- LSU issued a broadcast e-mail asking for beds for an increasing number of emergency personnel. Within hours, more than 2,000 air mattresses were donated.
- University Recreation waived all fees for evacuees on campus who wanted to use its facilities (including its indoor track, swimming pool, and climbing wall).
- The LSU Child Care Center provided free babysitting services to newly enrolled student parents from the evacuated areas.

LSU POLICE DEPARTMENT: ABOVE AND BEYOND

To maintain relief operations, the men and women of the LSU Police Department had to be even more than police officers at this time. Between 16- to 20-hour shifts, they slept in their stations in order to remain at hand. One supervisor commented that her officers filled their roles completely and were phenomenal in all the tasks they were asked to complete, even those that did not fall within their job descriptions. The police force was required to continue carrying out its first mission of keeping the university and its students safe while at the same time contributing to relief efforts including coordinating buses, securing triage areas, securing the field hospital and the special-needs shelter, directing traffic, and operating a command post inside the field hospital.

> "They needed food, water, a bathroom, and an ear."
>
> —LSU POLICE OFFICER ON THE EVACUEES ARRIVING ON CAMPUS

The police department worked with the LSU Athletic Department to make bus drop-off points as stress-free as possible for evacuees. Buses of evacuees would be brought to Alex Box Stadium (the university's varsity baseball venue), where passengers were given a place to rest and those who needed help were triaged. Bandaged evacuees struggled to walk under the weight of overflowing backpacks filled with what remained of their worldly possessions.

Only those who needed medical help, either at the field hospital or at the special-needs shelter, could remain on campus, as facilities were not available to shelter the general population. This created some discord initially, as some evacuees who had been rescued from their homes had been left in the hot sun on the interstate and deprived of basic needs for days before arriving at LSU. Telling them their miserable journey was not yet over required sensitivity.

LSU Police offered evacuees food, water, and restrooms as they stepped onto campus. Above all, LSU Police realized that many evacuees needed to talk of their devastation before they could focus clearly on their new situations. As circumstances allowed, officers listened to evacuees who needed to talk. LSU police said that once the evacuees' basic needs were satisfied, they could not have been more cooperative and considerate, even as they fled their homes and all they knew for points unknown.

The National Guard was called in to serve both on campus and in the surrounding community. In the weeks following Katrina, more than 300 National Guard members aided in security and other matters at LSU to relieve some of the burden that had been placed on LSU Police. The first group to arrive was the 438th Military Police Company from Kentucky, soon followed by guardsmen from the Virgin Islands, Connecticut, and other units from around the United States.

DISCUSSING HEALTH

A visit by the U.S. surgeon general, the U.S. secretary of Health and Human Services, and the director of the Centers for Disease Control and Prevention (CDC) highlighted the press conferences for the day, and LSU held a media briefing to provide information on campus protocols concerning the dignitary call. The LSU Office of Public Affairs had a representative of the U.S. Department of Health and Human Services (HSS) on hand to answer questions at an afternoon press conference, as well as members of the U.S. Public Health Service. A representative from the LSU Police Department addressed the media on campus security issues.

That afternoon, HHS secretary Mike Leavitt, CDC director Julie Gerberding, Surgeon General Richard Carmona, and several other officials arrived to tour areas where relief efforts were being carried out on campus. This team of health care, public health, and social service leaders came to LSU on a mission to extend care and services to Hurricane Katrina evacuees. The team built upon existing state, local, and federal efforts to provide for the immediate health care needs of evacuees by extending support to meet medical, mental health, and social services needs and to help ensure public health and prevent the spread of disease. The chancellor accompanied the officials on their tour of the facilities.

This visit came as the floodwaters left by Hurricane Katrina continued to stagnate, and fear in the community was palpable. Questions were raised about the possible spread of diseases, such as tetanus, West Nile virus, cholera, hepati-

Emergency relief workers used the tent city established at LSU's South Campus, about 3.5 miles from the main campus, as a meeting and dispatch center.

Jim Zietz/LSU Office of Public Affairs

tis, tuberculosis, and dysentery. The LSU Hurricane Information Center also fielded calls about unfounded rumors of a possible quarantine of the Baton Rouge area.

After touring the facilities, the officials held a press conference at the entrance of the field hospital to discuss LSU's role in the relief effort as well as their own mission to aid the people of the Gulf Coast.

A TENT CITY BASE OF OPERATIONS

In response to the need for shelter for emergency personnel, a tent city was erected at LSU's South Campus. For three weeks, until the winds of Hurricane Rita damaged it, this area would serve as a place for emergency personnel to gather, receive orders, and debrief. Emergency workers from across the nation who had come to Louisiana to help the state's residents in their time of need used this location as their temporary home between missions.

10

SEVENTH DAY OUT

MONDAY, SEPTEMBER 5, 2005

- The LSU football team filled an 18-wheel trailer with clothing, shoes, linens, pillows, toys, and books to take to a local shelter for Katrina survivors. All items came from LSU football players.
- LSU quarterback JaMarcus Russell hosted music legend and New Orleans evacuee Fats Domino in his off-campus apartment for days.

FLEXIBLE PLANS, ACADEMIC AND ATHLETIC

With classes due to resume the following day, university staff began to review how the academic schedule would need to be revised. The calendar was modified to accommodate the week of canceled classes, pushing most deadlines in the semester back one week. The university posted the new calendar on the LSU Web site and broadcast the calendar to the university community by e-mail.

Because of the continuing relief efforts on campus, the football game between LSU and Arizona State University that had been scheduled for September 10 in Tiger Stadium was moved to Tempe, Arizona. The athletic venues on campus were playing a central role in medical services, making it nearly impossible to have the game at home.

"There are considerable logistical issues that either affect the execution of a football game, or detract from providing recovery services in this time of need," said the chancellor in a press release. "We have collected as much information as possible and deliberated this issue carefully over the weekend, but the myriad of details and questions that remain unresolved dictate this move."

"We certainly need to support the medical services, and there is no indication that they will diminish in the days ahead."

—LSU ATHLETIC DIRECTOR ON RELOCATING THE LSU–ARIZONA STATE FOOTBALL GAME TO TEMPE

The intensity of medical recovery activity in the athletics facilities would be an obstacle for fans attending the game; all parking lots north of Tiger Stadium would probably be unavailable, and traffic could be even more congested than usual because of the number of medical personnel and evacuees who would still be on campus by the time of the game.

Another significant issue was the lack of available hotel rooms for the Arizona State football team and traveling

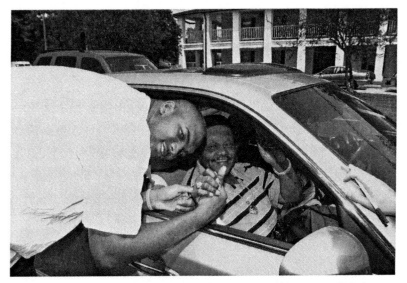

After Katrina, LSU quarterback JaMarcus Russell (left) opened his off-campus apartment to more than 20 people, including Fats Domino (right). The New Orleans music legend stayed with Russell for two days before being reunited with his family.

Steve Franz/LSU Sports Information

party, Southeastern Conference game officials, and members of the ESPN television crew. LSU officials advised fans that hotels were booked, and evacuees from the southeast Louisiana parishes had the highest priority.

The university and the athletic department also had to consider that medical and security personnel who were usually readily available for home football games were currently assisting in hurricane relief efforts and would not be able to provide their services at the game.

A CHANGED CAMPUS

Broadcast e-mails informed both established and displaced students on the current state of the campus. The provost sent a "welcome back" e-mail with several advisories to LSU students. She expressed concern and support for the entire student body, stating that "we understand that the past week has been exceptionally challenging for many of you. Please know that LSU faculty and staff are ready to get back to educational pursuits, and are prepared for the many questions and concerns that you will bring with you."

Concerns that she addressed included academic issues, traffic and parking, housing, security issues, student life, and volunteering. The e-mail informed students of the academic schedule changes as well as changes in the campus in general. In response to security concerns raised by parents as well as students, the provost informed students that LSU Police continued to do an exceptional job of maintaining a safe campus throughout the tragedy. She advised students that uniformed officers would be present on campus as part of the effort to aid hurricane evacuees and that students could expect to see various police officers on campus, as well as members of the National Guard and the U.S. Border Patrol. She thanked students who had volunteered and apprised all students of continuing opportunities to volunteer in the relief effort.

To reinforce the provost's message, a broadcast e-mail was sent from the Office of the University Registrar to advise faculty and students to check their class rosters. To provide for 2,800 newly registered students, special accommodations had been made. Classrooms, sections, and other class details had to be changed.

Later that day, an e-mail about the changes in the parking and traffic arrangements on campus was disseminated. Various emergency personnel were using several parking lots throughout campus to stage relief efforts, and a number of streets were open only to emergency personnel. One of the main streets leading into campus had been designated an ambulance corridor for several days. These issues were significant because a large number of LSU students drive to campus, and several commuter lots were closed.

The Office of Parking, Traffic, and Transportation issued a broadcast e-mail requesting that students, staff, and faculty minimize the number of vehicles on campus by taking buses, carpooling, bicycling, and walking.

11

EIGHTH DAY OUT
TUESDAY, SEPTEMBER 6, 2005

- Classes resumed at LSU for the first time since Friday, August 26.

- The Center for Academic Success developed a student workshop called *Beyond Survival: Thriving Academically after Katrina.*

- The *Daily Reveille* published a special post-Katrina edition the day students returned to classes. It had to be printed in Memphis because of hurricane damage at its usual printing facility in Hattiesburg, Mississippi.

BACK TO SCHOOL

By the time classes resumed on Tuesday, little of the LSU campus remained the way students had left it before the suspension of classes for Hurricane Katrina. Although there was minimal physical damage to campus, there were now new faces in classes. There were helicopters flying overhead, stopping only to unload their cargo of the infirm, some of whom had been plucked from rooftop islands in the middle of a sea that had once been their neighborhood. Military personnel walked alongside students strolling to class. But life was moving on, and as LSU officials worked to put the campus back in order, they asked students to help do the same.

> **"One of my professors asked for displaced students to raise their hands. There were so many. They weren't on TV anymore; they were in my classroom."**
>
> **—LSU STUDENT**

Because of the influx of students displaced by Katrina, class size became a major issue for the university. Seminars that were once a comfortable size quadrupled. The day before classes resumed, LSU had registered 1,454 of the 3,285 students from hurricane-affected areas who would register by the deadline. Four hundred more were admitted the following day but had not yet registered for class.

To keep class sizes reasonable and classes available, university officials put out a call for instructors willing to teach classes to handle the demand. In a matter of days, 700 faculty members from universities and colleges in areas affected by Katrina responded, along with a large number from around the country who were willing to help. Even after the high volume of responses forced the notice to be removed from the LSU Web site, calls continued to come from interested instructors offering their services.

Many of the calls the Hurricane Information Center received pertained to when classes would resume and how displaced students would go about enrolling at LSU, but as the deadline for enrollment drew near, these questions became moot. As volunteers' energies were needed back at their regular positions within the university, the hours of the call center were reduced. But the center had served its purpose. Volunteers took more than 6,000 calls during the 13 days the call center was operational. And many who didn't phone the hotline turned to the university's online information center, which detailed LSU's role in everything from resettling displaced students to sheltering lost pets. By Tuesday, just nine days after Katrina, page views of the Web site totaled nearly a million.

LSU FOUNDATION CREATES STUDENT RELIEF FUND

Hurricane Katrina virtually destroyed seven parishes in south Louisiana, three counties in Mississippi, and two counties in Alabama. Nearly 7,000 LSU students called the devastated parishes home, and now more than 3,000 hurricane-affected students had transferred to LSU after suffer-

Biological sciences sophomore Matt Giglia volunteered with some of his Sigma Phi Epsilon fraternity brothers to collect supplies outside the PMAC.

Jolie Duhon/*Daily Reveille*

ing financial hardship and property loss. To assist these students, the LSU Foundation established an account dedicated to the student relief efforts.

The goal of the program is to assist students who have lost financial support or have been displaced by Hurricane Katrina or, later, Hurricane Rita. The fund would aid LSU students from the affected areas as well as students from other affected universities who were admitted to LSU after Katrina hit. In an effort to handle all applications with the utmost compassion for individual needs, the LSU Office of Student Aid and Scholarships developed a system to ensure that aid would be disbursed to the students who were most adversely affected. As fund-raising efforts continued, additional awards could be made throughout the year.

HOME IS NOT ALWAYS WHERE THE HEART IS

The relief fund, however, could not help the new students with finding housing. Apartments and hotels were still booked solid with evacuees from New Orleans, and many of the students enrolling at LSU had no one in Baton Rouge with whom they could board. That left the burden for housing on the university itself. The Friday before classes resumed, the chancellor announced that any student applying for housing would be accommodated.

By Monday, September 5, it had become clear that the chancellor had underestimated the demand. An announcement was posted on the LSU Web site stating that housing was no longer available on campus. However, students were still arriving at LSU ready to register, many of them with everything they owned in a suitcase.

To alleviate the problem, staff members of the Office of the University Registrar and the Office of Undergraduate

Admissions began calling area churches looking for rooms. They gave students directions to various student centers on campus and called anyone they thought might be able to help. Students were also referred to shareyourhome.org, a Web site started by an LSU alumnus that listed individuals willing to open their homes to those in need of a place to stay.

12

NINTH DAY OUT

WEDNESDAY, SEPTEMBER 7, 2005

- Twenty-three percent of LSU's student body hails from the seven most devastated parishes in the Louisiana.

THE CALM AFTER THE STORM

The campus continued moving toward normalcy as students fell back into their daily routines of attending classes and looking forward to the season's first football game. And for the most part, the campus looked a lot like its former self, save for a line of students stretching back the length of a football field from the site of the temporary registration center.

For the rest of that first week of school following Katrina, displaced students continued to be admitted. By the end of the process, 3,285 new students had been admitted in 10 days.

RULES WERE MADE TO BE BROKEN

During the admissions process, LSU's Office of the University Registrar added new sections of courses, moved courses into bigger classrooms, assigned faculty members to teach courses for affected students, and assisted with any other issues related to classes and schedules. Because there was no precedent for this tragedy, it stood to reason that flexibility and creativity would be needed to handle the influx of students. So the registrar's office bent rules and ultimately broke a few in the process. Students evacuating had left home thinking they would only be gone for a few days, not knowing what would become of their homes and colleges. As a result, many of the official papers they would need to enroll in a new school were gone. With this in mind, LSU admissions staff asked displaced students seeking enrollment to present at least a valid student identification card from their institutions to complete the admissions process. But in some cases, even that was not possible.

> **"We had students lined up in the hallway, up the stairs, and down the second floor hallway waiting to enter and get registered. Every student brought with them a different set of circumstances, issues, or problems that we worked through one at a time."**
>
> **—ASSOCIATE REGISTRAR**

Some of the students admitted to LSU from other institutions were enrolled without true credentials because they were unobtainable (in many cases they were underwater). New students were put into full classes, prerequisites were overlooked, courses were added, and both faculty and classrooms were changed to accommodate the new and larger classes. All of these were steps LSU would not normally have taken, but at the time, it was what was needed. That LSU, a large institution with rules and red tape like any other, bent rules was a sign of just how much upheaval Katrina had brought even to those areas not directly affected by the winds and storm surges she carried with her.

WWL LEAVES CAMPUS

As more and more students were coming onto campus, one group was leaving. Katrina had forced New Orleans television station WWL to relocate to the Manship School of Mass Communication on the LSU campus. For nearly a week, some 100 WWL employees used the university's facilities while the station continued to cover events back in New Orleans. After leaving LSU, WWL moved its operations to the studios of the local PBS affiliate, WLPB. While at LSU, WWL provided a service to students here by broadcasting stories shot and produced by LSU's student-run Tiger TV.

WWL would later donate $60,000 to the Manship School to fund a new professorship.

THE FINAL PUSH

Volunteer operations were beginning to wind down, and faculty and staff members were returning to their normal duties. The Hurricane Information Center had decreased its hours again to those of a regular workday. Slowly, the routine of university life was resuming, albeit with more than 2,800 new students.

Yet the following Saturday, September 10, there would be a reminder of how different everyone's lives had become, as LSU's football team played what would have been its second home game on the road in Tempe, Arizona, against Arizona State University.

For that night, the end zones at Sun Devil Stadium had been painted with the Web site address of the Katrina Student Relief Fund (katrinaSRF.com), and a video of the chancellor was aired over the stadium's Jumbotron. It had been recorded a couple days earlier in a small studio in the Office of Public Affairs, and it would mark the first time the nation as a whole was able to hear the "voice" of LSU address what had been taking place on campus for the past several days.

Chancellor O'Keefe closed his message by saying that LSU had done and would continue to do everything it could

The Arizona State Sun Devils, LSU's first opponent of the football season, generously donated $1 million to relief efforts. Half of that amount went to the Katrina Student Relief Fund, and the remaining $500,000 went to the Bush-Clinton Hurricane Katrina Fund.

Steve Franz/LSU Sports Information

for the people of Louisiana. But the time had come for others to help, and the Katrina Student Relief Fund could help them do so.

With 1:13 remaining on the clock that night, LSU scored a touchdown that ultimately put Arizona State away and gave the Tigers their first win of the season. LSU fans cheered in Tempe and back in Baton Rouge, where thousands had gathered in Tiger Stadium to watch the game on large projection screens set up on the field. Despite the loss,

Arizona State generously donated $500,000 of the proceeds from that night's ticket sales to the Katrina Student Relief Fund.

That Saturday night, for the first time since Katrina, the mood lightened on campus. In more ways than one, LSU was not beaten, and neither was Louisiana. Recovery was far from over, but there was hope that things would soon be better.

EPILOGUE

Over the years, there have been a great number of triumphs under the roof of LSU's Pete Maravich Assembly Center (PMAC). Shaquille O'Neal once captivated his fellow students and the local community with his playing abilities in that building. The president of the United States addressed a packed arena of students, parents, and faculty members gathered for a recent spring commencement ceremony. But nature provided the arena with its greatest triumph to date when civilian volunteers joined medical and military personnel from around the country to aid Hurricane Katrina evacuees within its walls.

In a mind-boggling four days, the facility became an 800-bed field hospital. Where people had once cheered themselves hoarse in anticipation of the final buzzer for a basketball game, in the aftermath of Katrina there were entirely different sounds: doctors and nurses calling out for medical supplies, sobbing patients, religious leaders praying aloud with those who understandably felt that the world had come to an end.

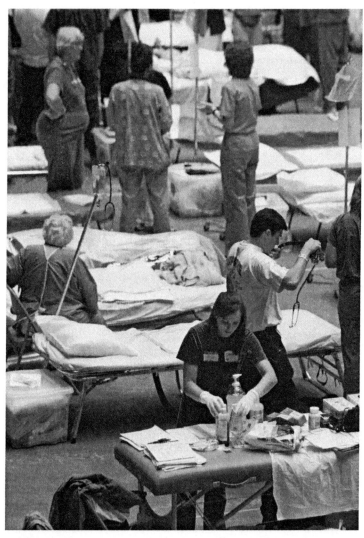

More than 1,700 medical personnel from across the country addressed the needs of citizens affected by Hurricane Katrina.

On Thursday, September 8, 2005, the building began to grow quiet as the hospital closed. In all, 6,000 patients had been cared for inside the PMAC. Fifteen thousand had been sent on to shelters and other special-needs facilities. More than 2,000 prescriptions were filled at LSU because many people who had evacuated had also lost contact with their doctors and pharmacists after the storm. More than 1,700 volunteer medical personnel came to the LSU campus from Louisiana, Washington, D.C., Georgia, Arkansas, Mississippi, Florida, Texas, Utah, Arizona, Illinois, and Washington state. All were part of the largest deployment of public health officials in the nation's history.

With the hospital closing, the impetus shifted to the needs of the student body, particularly those who had been recently admitted from areas affected by Katrina. LSU Mental Health Service staff continued meeting with students, going to the residence halls for counseling sessions and seminars. In addition, the Wellness Education Department, in conjunction with the Mental Health Service, cofacilitated a series of discussion sessions titled "Coping with Katrina." The people of Louisiana, Mississippi, and Alabama will cope with the aftermath of Katrina for years to come.

We learned many lessons at LSU in our hurricane recovery effort. In a less-than-ideal world, we would encourage other colleges and universities to learn from our recent experiences and consider the following.

- Remember that communication is key.
- Have detailed disaster and campus evacuation plans in place.
- Use campus resources already in place to assist with these crisis plans.
- Remember that the best-laid plans require flexibility and creativity, as glitches will inevitably arise.
- Know what your facilities can accommodate in terms of additional people, emergency vehicles, and temporary structures. If you are located in an area prone to particular types of natural disasters, at the beginning of each semester give students a list of items they should not be without in the event of such a disaster. (In hurricane-prone areas, these items might include a flashlight, batteries, bottled water, and a battery-operated radio.)
- Identify all qualified media personnel on campus (perhaps from a journalism department or mass communications program) and have them on an emergency list for times of crisis.
- Be flexible with scheduling issues.
- Communicate with your students, but don't flood their

inboxes with e-mails, as important information may be
overlooked.

- Think of materials your Public Affairs team and qualified
  emergency professionals might need in times of crisis,
  such as badges and T-shirts. Have these ready to go.
- Know which of your faculty members have expertise in
  which types of crisis management and be able to call upon
  them on short notice.
- Identify members of your community who would be willing to house students and emergency workers. Establish a
  database with their contact information.
- Develop courses that could easily go online in the event of
  short-term or long-term school closings due to a disaster.
- Consider remote servers for key university information.
- Never underestimate the rallying power and strength
  of the volunteers on your campus, in the community at
  large, and around our great nation. Do not waste any time
  in mobilizing them.
- Encourage a service-oriented student body with service-
  learning programs on campus and freshman reading se-
  lections that give birth to public outreach.

As fate would have it, just weeks before the storm, LSU's incoming freshman had been assigned Tracy Kidder's *Moun-*

tains beyond Mountains: The Quest of Dr. Paul Farmer, A Man Who Would Cure the World as required summer reading. The book chronicles Dr. Farmer's work with an impoverished, sick, and suffering population in Haiti and Peru.

At an academic convocation on August 19, Kidder and Dr. Farmer addressed the more than 4,000 readers at the Carl Maddox Field House. "I am really excited when I think about where you guys are going and what you could do in the world," Kidder said to the crowd.

A mere 10 days later, most of the audience would be applying what they had learned as they comforted the impoverished, sick, and suffering survivors of Katrina in the very room in which they had heard Kidder and Farmer speak.

Students often see college as a dress rehearsal for life. Perhaps the greatest lesson we learned from Katrina is that there are no dress rehearsals; the best way to get the most difficult jobs done is for hope and humanity to join hands. In the wake of Katrina, we at LSU had a front-row seat on the beauty of that union as it carried us through each difficult day. May it continue to carry us all down the long and winding road to recovery.

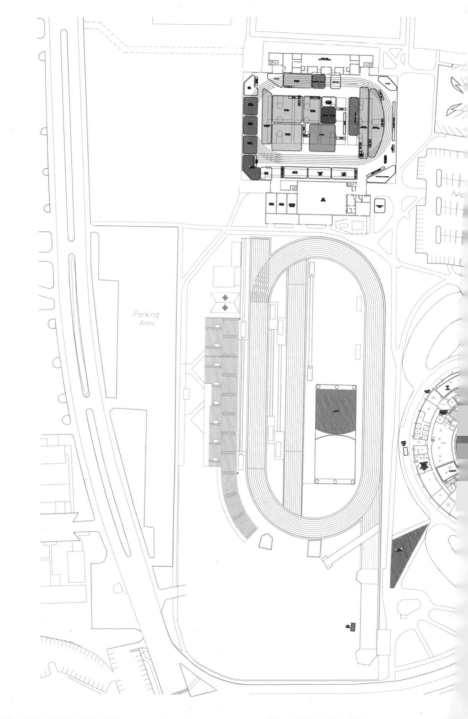

Parking
Area

Empowered by the Spirit
Campus Ministry Faces the Future

**A Pastoral Letter on
Campus Ministry**

November 15, 1985
National Conference of Catholic Bishops

Following the bishops' November 1982 general meeting, the Committee on Education was commissioned to draft a pastoral letter on campus ministry. The first draft of this letter was submitted to the bishops in June 1985. The Administrative Committee placed the subsequent draft, *Empowered by the Spirit: Campus Ministry Faces the Future,* on the bishops' November 1985 agenda. Approval of the text was given during the plenary assembly of the National Conference of Catholic Bishops in Washington, D.C., November 15, 1985. Accordingly, publication of this pastoral letter is authorized by the undersigned.

Monsignor Daniel F. Hoye
General Secretary
December 13, 1985   NCCB/USCC

Scripture texts used in this work are taken from the *New American Bible,* copyright © 1970, by the Confraternity of Christian Doctrine, Washington, D.C., and are used by permission of copyright owner. All rights reserved.

Excerpts from *The Documents of Vatican II,* edited by Walter M. Abbott, SJ, copyright © 1966. Reprinted with permission of America Press, Inc., New York, N.Y.

Contents

Introduction

1. "I pray that he will bestow on you gifts in keeping with the riches of his glory. May he strengthen you inwardly through the working of his Spirit. May Christ dwell in your hearts through faith and may charity be the root and foundation of your life" (Eph 3:16-17). For over a century, Catholic campus ministry in our country, empowered by the Spirit, has been forming communities of faith which witness to the presence of the risen Christ. Now we are at the beginning of a new era filled with opportunities to build up the faith community on campuses and to promote the well-being of higher education and society as a whole. In this pastoral letter addressed to the Catholic Church in the United States and especially to the Church on campus, we offer our prayerful support, encouragement, and guidance to the men and women who are committed to bringing the message of Christ to the academic world. In preparing this letter, we have consulted with many of them and have come to a deeper appreciation of their dedication and achievements, as well as their concerns and frustrations. This new era, which is filled with promise, challenges campus ministry to respond creatively to the promptings of the Spirit for the well-being of the Church and higher education.

2. Our 1981 statement on Catholic higher education concluded by noting "the excellent intellectual and pastoral leadership of many Catholics engaged as teachers, administrators, and campus ministers in the colleges and universities which are not Catholic."[1] We said at that time that "we hope for a future opportunity to speak of their invaluable contribution to the intellectual life of our country."[2] In

---

1. "Catholic Higher Education and the Pastoral Mission of the Church," in *Pastoral Letters of the United States Catholic Bishops,* 4 vols., ed. Hugh J. Nolan (Washington, D.C.: USCC Office of Publishing and Promotion Services, 1983-84), vol. 4, 1975-1983, no. 64, footnote 32. (Hereafter all pastoral letters will be cited from the Nolan text.)
2. Ibid.

this pastoral letter, we fulfill that hope and turn our attention primarily to the ministry of the Church on these public and private campuses, where each year millions of Catholics are being prepared as future leaders of society and Church.[3] We are mindful of our previous comments on the crucial importance of Catholic higher education, especially the distinctive task of campus ministry on Catholic campuses to call the total institution to spread the Gospel and to preserve and enrich its religious traditions.[4] In addition, the suggestions for this document made by those who serve at Catholic institutions affirmed that all who minister in the world of higher education have certain common concerns and similar desires for cooperation. Collaboration among all colleges and universities within a diocese enhances the Church's ministry to higher education. Mutual support, joint sponsorship of programs, and sharing of resources improve the total efforts of campus ministry. Many of the perspectives, suggestions, and directions in this pastoral letter should be helpful to those who serve so well in our Catholic institutions of higher education.

3. Campus ministry is best understood in its historical, sociological, and theological context. Thus, the first section discusses our hopes for the Church on campus in the light of its previous history. The next section locates campus ministry within the relationship between the Church and the world of higher education, highlighting the need for renewed dialogue. Campus ministry derives its life from the persons who bring the Gospel of Christ to the academic world. Therefore, the third section focuses on the members of the Church on campus, emphasizing the call of all the baptized to collaborate in the work of the Church, as well as the special responsibility of professional campus ministers to empower others for this task. The fourth section examines six aspects of campus ministry that flow from the nature of the Church and the situation on campus. Here we state principles and suggest strategies for carrying out this ministry. The epilogue notes our own responsibilities as bishops to serve the Church on campus and calls the Church to an exciting new phase in the history of campus ministry in our country.

---

3. There are over 3,300 institutions of higher learning in the United States. The 1985 fall enrollment was 12,247,000 of which approximately 9.6 million attend public colleges and universities and 2.7 million attend private institutions. In the total student population, 43% are 25 or older and 45% attend part time. In recent times Catholics have constituted around 39% of the freshman class. For these statistics, see *Chronicle of Higher Education,* September 4, 1985.

4. "Catholic Higher Education," nos. 45-46.

I. History and Current Opportunities

A. History and Contemporary Developments

4. The Church's response to current opportunities on campus will benefit from an awareness of the history of the Newman Movement in the United States.[5] This ministry began in 1883 at the University of Wisconsin with the founding, through lay initiative, of the Melvin Club which was designed to keep Catholics on campus in touch with their religious heritage. A decade later the first Newman Club was established at the University of Pennsylvania, with much the same purpose. It was named after John Henry Cardinal Newman, who was the English leader in the nineteenth-century intellectual renewal in the Church and later was chosen the great patron of campus ministers in our country. During this initial stage, farsighted leaders recognized that the growing number of Catholic collegians attending public institutions needed support and instruction in their religious heritage. They responded by establishing clubs for Catholic students, with their own chaplains and residence halls.

5. In 1908, the second stage began with the establishment of the first association of Catholic clubs in state universities. What would become the National Newman Club Federation replaced this first effort about the time of World War I. This phase, which lasted until 1969, was often characterized by a defensive and even hostile attitude on the part of Catholic students and their chaplains toward the academic world, which was perceived as dominated by a secularist philosophy. During this period, many students and chaplains in the Newman Movement felt estranged from the rest of the Church and decried the lack of support from the hierarchy.

---

5. See John Whitney Evans, *The Newman Movement* (Notre Dame: University of Notre Dame Press, 1980).

6. The third stage, begun in 1969 in response to the Second Vatican Council and continuing until the present, has produced some healthy new developments. First, the Church as a whole has grown in appreciation and support of campus ministry. It is true there are still problems: some colleges and universities lack officially appointed campus ministers and many others are understaffed and suffer from financial problems. At times, there are misunderstandings between the Church on campus and local parishes and diocesan offices. However, progress has clearly been made in integrating campus ministry into the life of the Church. Today, there are over two thousand Catholics ministering on campuses throughout the country—a significant increase over a couple of decades ago. There is an increased commitment to providing well-trained campus ministers who appreciate the need for continued professional and theological development. Student groups at all levels collaborate with official representatives of the Church. Diocesan directors of campus ministry help keep campus concerns before the whole Church. More Catholics appreciate the importance of campus ministry and support diocesan funding of this work. Through this pastoral letter, we affirm these positive developments and pledge to work with others to build on them. We bring to the attention of the whole Church the importance of campus ministry for the future well-being of the Church and society. Our goal is to foster a closer relationship and a greater spirit of cooperation between campus ministry and the rest of the local Church. Campus ministry is an integral part of the Church's mission to the world and must be seen in that light.

7. Second, we endorse the improving relationship between the Church on campus and the academic community. While problems remain, Catholics have developed a greater understanding of the positive values and legitimate concerns of higher education. Many campus ministers have established good working relationships with administrators, faculty, and staff. There is greater appreciation of the way the Church benefits from the teaching, research, and service carried on by colleges and universities. Similarly, many administrators view campus ministry as an ally in the common effort to provide an integrated learning experience for the students. Faculty members frequently value the presence of campus ministers who demonstrate an appreciation of the spiritual life and can articulate their Catholic heritage. In our consultations, we found that many leaders in the academic community welcome a word from the Church on matters of mutual concern.[6] Our hope in this letter is to build on this fund of

---

6. Among the many consultations with administrators, faculty, students, selected experts, and others, we found especially helpful the close to 300 responses received

good will and to heal any wounds which linger from past mistakes and misunderstandings. With respect for the freedom and autonomy of the academic community, we believe it is time to foster a renewed dialogue between the Church and higher education, to the benefit of society as a whole.

8. Third, we affirm the development of ecumenical and interfaith relationships. There are, of course, problems in resolving longstanding differences, and at some colleges and universities dialogue and cooperation have been difficult to establish and maintain. However, on many campuses, the Catholic community and other religious groups who share a common vision of ministry and who are interested in ecumenical and interfaith cooperation have developed strong working relationships. This occurs especially with other Christian Churches, with whom we share a common commitment to Jesus Christ, and with the Jewish community, with whom we hold a common heritage and shared Scriptures. In some situations, Catholic campus ministers share an interfaith center and collaborate in some ministerial tasks. In other places, the Catholic community cooperates with other religious groups through regular meetings, joint study, and shared prayer. Mutual trust has grown as members of various religious traditions work together on common programs, such as projects to promote social justice. We commend this ecumenical and interfaith progress and give full support to greater and more creative efforts in this direction. Catholics who are deeply rooted in their tradition and who maintain a strong sense of identity with their religious heritage will be better prepared to carry out this mission. We appreciate the contributions and cooperative attitudes of most of the various religious communities on campus. The Catholic community on campus might also seek to engage those who are concerned with human ethical values of our society but do not directly relate their concerns to a faith tradition. To those who demonstrate less tolerant attitudes, we extend an invitation to join in the dialogue. In this pastoral message, we address the Catholic campus community and discuss its particular challenges and opportunities. While we will not treat directly the ecumenical and interfaith dimensions of campus ministry today, we hope that the Catholic communities on individual campuses will be prompted by this letter to renewed dialogue and collaboration in serving the common good.

9. Finally, this third stage in the history of the Newman Movement has produced a remarkable diversity of legitimate styles and approaches to campus ministry, designed to match available resources with the

---

from presidents and elected faculty leaders representing institutions of higher education from all 50 states who informed us of their hopes and concerns.

unique situations at particular colleges and universities. These creative responses range from well-organized teams serving the needs of a large university parish to an individual ministering part time in a small community college. The styles include ministries that are primarily sacramental and those that rely mainly on the ministry of presence. Some campus ministers work on Catholic campuses where they can influence policy decisions, while others serve in public institutions where they have little or no access to the centers of power. In some situations priests are working full time, while in others the ministry is carried out almost entirely by members of religious orders and lay people. Ministers on residential campuses can offer many set programs for students, while those who serve on commuter campuses must be attentive to the creative possibilities demanded by such a fluid situation. Most serve on one campus, although some are responsible for several colleges and universities. While we cannot discuss in detail all styles of ministry, we will offer principles and strategies designed to encourage all those concerned with the Church on campus to make vigorous and creative applications to their own situations.

B. Current Challenges and Opportunities

10. We believe this is the opportune time to address a challenging word to the Church on campus. Catholics are attending colleges and universities in numbers that far exceed their percentage of the general population.[7] It is crucial that these emerging leaders of Church and society be exposed to the best of our Catholic tradition and encounter dedicated leaders who will share their journey of faith with them. Thus, the time is right to encourage campus ministers to renew their own spiritual lives and to facilitate the faith development of the Catholics on campus.

11. Today, there is a growing interest among many Catholics in various ministries. On campus, there is a great reservoir of energy and talent that could be utilized in the service of the Church and the world. Therefore, the time is right to challenge faculty members, administrators, support staff, and students to contribute their time and gifts to the common effort to help the academic community achieve its goals and to build up the Church on campus.

---

7. In both 1983 and 1984, 39.3% of college freshmen were Roman Catholic. See Alexander W. Astin, *The American Freshman National Norms for Fall 1983* (and *1984*), published by the American Council on Education and the University of California at Los Angeles. Catholics constitute about 25% of the general population in the United States.

6

12. The academic world is in the midst of an important debate on how to improve the quality of higher education in our country.[8] Fundamental questions about the purpose, methods, and direction of higher education must be addressed, as colleges and universities continue to define their mission and to improve their performance. Therefore, the time is right to encourage Catholics on campus to participate in these local debates and, thus, to contribute their insights and values to this crucial national discussion.

8. Cf. "Involvement in Learning: Realizing the Potential of American Education" (National Institute of Education, 1984); William J. Bennett, "To Reclaim a Legacy" (National Endowment for the Humanities, 1984); "Integrity in the College Curriculum: A Report to the Academic Community" (Association of American Colleges, 1985); and "Higher Education and the American Resurgence" (Carnegie Foundation for the Advancement of Teaching, 1985).

II. Campus Ministry and the Relationship between the Church and Higher Education

---

A. History

13. Campus ministry is an expression of the Church's special desire to be present to all who are involved in higher education. Throughout its history, the Church has been instrumental in cultivating the intellectual life. During the period of the Fathers, great centers of learning at Antioch and Alexandria instructed the faithful and promoted the integration of faith and culture. The Church contributed her resources to the task of forming medieval universities and founded many of them, including the great schools of Bologna, Paris, Oxford, and Cambridge. In the modern world, government increasingly has taken over the responsibility for higher education, with a resulting split between the Church and the university. This has occurred in our own country with the establishment of a massive system of public higher education that has its own autonomy. Shortly after 1900, it was evident that enrollments in this system were growing faster than those in the Catholic and Protestant colleges, which for so long had constituted higher education in the United States. From the perspective of faith, Christians often detected in public institutions a growing secularism that celebrated the autonomy of reason and left little room for consideration of religious questions or moral values. This situation intensified after World War I, and the Church responded not only by increasing her traditional commitment to higher education, but also by trying to protect Catholic students from the antireligious elements perceived on public campuses. During this period, the Church and higher education experienced a good deal of mutual misunderstanding. Some people in the academic world feared that the Church would try to reassert, in more subtle ways, its control over higher education. On the other side, members of the Church, at times, regarded secular higher education as a threat to the Christian way of life. The time has come to move beyond these misunderstandings and to forge a new relationship between the Church and higher education that respects the unique character of each. We remain convinced that "cooperation between these two great institutions, Church and university, is indispensable to the health of society."[9]

B. The Contribution of Higher Education

14. We respect the autonomy of the academic community and appreciate its great contributions to the common good. Higher education benefits the human family through its research, which expands our common pool of knowledge. By teaching people to think critically and to search for the truth, colleges and universities help to humanize our world. The collegiate experience provides individuals with attitudes and skills that can be used in productive work, harmonious living, and responsible citizenship. Since higher education in the United States has taken on public service as one of its tasks, society has received significant assistance in solving human and technical problems. The Second Vatican Council placed this contribution in a personal context when it said that people who apply themselves to philosophy, history, science, and the arts help "to elevate the human family to a more sublime understanding of truth, goodness, and beauty and to the formation of judgments which embody universal values."[10]

15. The Church, as well as society as a whole, benefits from the contributions of higher education. The members of the Church hold a common faith in Jesus Christ, a faith that seeks understanding. When the academic world produces new knowledge and encourages critical thinking, it assists Christians in the process of deepening and articulating their faith. When higher education fosters fidelity toward truth in scientific research and collaborative efforts to improve the quality of life in our world, it helps to prepare for the acceptance of the gospel message.[11]

9. "To Teach as Jesus Did: A Pastoral Message on Catholic Education," in *Pastoral Letters*, vol. 3, 1962-1974, no. 63.
10. "Pastoral Constitution on the Church in the Modern World," in *The Documents of Vatican II*, ed. Walter M. Abbott, SJ (New York: America Press, 1966), no. 57. (Hereafter all documents from Vatican II will be cited from the Abbott text.)
11. Ibid.

16. There is no doubt that the world of higher education has its own problems that must be addressed and dehumanizing practices that must be challenged. Fidelity to the Gospel demands critical judgment, as well as affirmation. It is, however, vital that campus ministry maintains a fundamental appreciation of the contributions made by higher education to society and the Church.

C. The Contribution of the Church

17. The Church brings to the dialogue with higher education its general mission to preach the Gospel of Christ and to help the human family achieve its full destiny.[12] Thus, the Church seeks to help higher education attain its lofty goal of developing a culture in which human beings can realize their full potential.[13] In providing this assistance, the Church joins its voice with others in promoting the ideal of educating the whole person. From our perspective, this means keeping the dignity and worth of human beings in the center of our reflections on the purpose of higher education. Education is the process by which persons are "assisted in the harmonious development of their physical, moral, and intellectual endowments."[14] It aims at the formation of individuals who have a sense of ultimate purpose and are moving toward greater freedom, maturity, and integration. At the same time, genuine education nurtures a sense of responsibility for the common good and provides skills for active involvement in community life.

18. We think that it is important to keep the problems of higher education in a larger societal and educational context. Thus, family life must be seen as central to the process of educating the whole person, since "the family is the first and fundamental school of social living."[15] Moreover, improvement in the quality of higher education is dependent on primary and secondary schools doing a better job of cultivating the intellect, passing on the cultural heritage, and fostering constructive values. If students are better prepared by a healthy family life and solid primary and secondary education, institutions of higher learning can attend to their primary purpose, "the passionate and disinterested search for the truth," which makes human

---

12. Ibid., no. 92.

13. "The Church of the University," *The Pope Speaks,* vol. 27, no. 3 (Fall 1982), p. 252.

14. "Declaration on Christian Education," in *Documents of Vatican II,* no. 1.

15. John Paul II, *On the Family* (Washington, D.C.: USCC Office of Publishing and Promotion Services, 1982), no. 37.

beings free and helps them achieve their full humanity in accord with their dignity and worth.[16] The search for truth should also include the ability to handle ethical issues and to achieve a harmonious integration of intellect and will.

19. The Church also brings to the dialogue its traditional understanding of wisdom. We believe that the faith community and the institutions of higher learning are involved in a common pursuit of the life of wisdom.[17] There are various interpretations of wisdom, but we agree with those who hold that its pursuit includes discovering the highest principles that integrate all knowledge; uncovering the deepest secrets that constitute human nature; and achieving a personal synthesis in which knowledge and love are ultimately united. For us, the mystery of human existence is fully revealed in Jesus Christ. He reminds us of our profound dignity and our immense potential. He provides us with perspective and teaches by example how love illumines knowledge. The wisdom that we learn from Christ includes the cross, which confounds the wisdom of the world (1 Cor 1:18-24). From the perspective of the cross, we are called to challenge the limitations and contradictions of the world (1 Cor 3:18-23). At the same time, our wisdom tradition includes an understanding of God's mysterious plan to bring all things in the heavens and on earth into unity under the headship of Christ (Eph 1:9-10). The risen Lord has poured out his Spirit on all creation and so we are moved to celebrate truth, goodness, and beauty wherever they are to be found. Since no single community can monopolize the gift of wisdom, the Church joins with the university and others in the search for wisdom. But, when the quest for wisdom is forgotten or diminished, then the Church must keep the ideal alive for the good of society. When the so-called wisdom of the world is employed in support of injustice, the Church must proclaim the wisdom of the cross, which challenges all oppressive structures. In the Church, the practical wisdom enunciated by the Hebrew sages is celebrated; the traditional philosophical wisdom is remembered; and the integrating wisdom of faith is proclaimed. For Christians, this whole quest for wisdom finds its summation and final fulfillment in Jesus Christ, who is the wisdom of God (1 Cor 1:24). We are convinced that the Christian wisdom synthesis, merely sketched out here, is a valuable resource in the continuing dialogue between the Church and higher education.

20. In a new relationship, the Church can work with higher education in improving the human community and establishing a culture that enables all human beings to reach their full potential. While admitting

---

16. "The Church of the University," p. 250.
17. Ibid., p. 252.

our failures in the past, we are concentrating on the future and a new era of cooperation. In the dialogue, we expect to learn and benefit from the work of higher education and will contribute our support, experience, and insights.

D. Campus Ministry Described and Defined

21. Campus ministry is one of the important ways the Church exercises her mission in higher education. Its goals include promoting theological study and reflection on the religious nature of human beings "so that intellectual, moral, and spiritual growth can proceed together; sustaining a Christian community on campus, with the pastoral care and liturgical worship it requires; integration of its apostolic ministry with other ministries of the local community and the diocese; and helping the Christian community on campus to serve its members and others, including the many nonstudents who gravitate toward the university."[18] Campus ministry gathers the Catholics on campus for prayer, worship, and learning in order that they might bring the light of the Gospel to illumine the concerns and hopes of the academic community. All the members of the Church on campus are called, according to their own gifts, to share in this ministry, guided by the professional campus ministers. "The work of campus ministry requires continual evaluation of traditional methods of ministry and also new approaches which are licitly and responsibly employed. These latter can be highly appropriate in the campus setting, where there exists an audience receptive to the kind of sound innovation which may in the future prove beneficial to the larger Catholic community."[19] Such creativity has produced great diversity in organization, style, and approach, as campus ministers strive to form a searching, believing, loving, worshipping Catholic presence on campus. With this diversity in mind, campus ministry can be defined as the public presence and service through which properly prepared baptized persons are empowered by the Spirit to use their talents and gifts on behalf of the Church in order to be sign and instrument of the kingdom in the academic world. The eye of faith discerns campus ministry where commitment to Christ and care for the academic world meet in purposeful activity to serve and realize the kingdom of God.

18. "To Teach as Jesus Did," no. 67.
19. Ibid., no. 69.

13

III. Persons Who Serve on Campus

A. The Baptized

22. The Church carries out its pastoral mission to the academic world both through its communal life and through the Christian witness of its individual members. "The baptized by the regeneration and the anointing of the Holy Spirit are consecrated as a spiritual house and a holy priesthood" (cf. 1 Pt 2:4-5), in order that through all their works they may "proclaim the power of Him who has called them out of darkness into His marvelous light."[20] All the faithful on campus, by virtue of their baptism, share in the task of bringing the humanizing light of the Gospel to bear on the life of the academic community. They are called to live out Christian values while engaging in the teaching, learning, research, public service, and campus life that constitutes the academic world. They are united with other believers in this work but make their own unique contributions, according to their personal talents and specific circumstances. "As generous distributors of God's manifold grace, put your gifts at the service of one another" (1 Pt 4:10). The Second Vatican Council further specified this scriptural teaching: "From the reception of these charisms or gifts, including those which are less dramatic, there arise for each believer the right and duty to use them in the Church and in the world for the good of [humankind] and for the upbuilding of the Church."[21] Thus, all the baptized members of the academic community have the opportunity and the obligation, according to their unique talents and situations, to join with others to help higher education reach its full potential.

---

20. "Dogmatic Constitution on the Church," in *Documents of Vatican II*, no. 10.
21. "Decree on the Apostolate of the Laity," in *Documents of Vatican II*, no. 3.

23. The faithful are called not only to bring Christian witness to the academic world, but also to exercise their baptismal prerogatives by helping to build up the Church on campus. While many persons today generously contribute their time, talent, and experience to the faith community, Catholic faculty, staff, and administration have a unique opportunity and calling to lead and direct campus ministry programs, according to their gifts. These individuals are particularly needed on the many campuses throughout the country where no campus ministry programs presently exist. This contribution is enhanced when individuals take time to prepare themselves through prayer and study for this work. In section four of this letter, perspectives and strategies will be enunciated to guide the various aspects of campus ministry. We hope that students, including the large number of older students,[22] administrators, faculty members, and all who are concerned with higher education will be able to make creative applications to their own situations based on the conviction that the Spirit moves among all the people of God, prompting them, according to their own talents, to discern anew the signs of the times and to interpret them boldly in the light of the faith.[23]

B. Professional Campus Ministers

24. Some members of the Church on campus are called to lead the faith community. Ideally, these men and women are professionally trained and exercise the kind of leadership that serves and empowers others. As officially appointed campus ministers, they are sent to form the faith community so that it can be a genuine sign and instrument of the kingdom. Their task is to identify, call forth, and coordinate the diverse gifts of the Spirit possessed by all the members of the faith community. Their challenge is to educate all the baptized to appreciate their own calls to service and to create a climate where initiative is encouraged and contributions are appreciated. One of the most important functions of campus ministers is to provide a vision and a sense of overall direction that will encourage and guide the other members to contribute to the well-being of the academic community and the Church on campus. If they understand their own family relationships in a faith perspective, they will be able to help others who are trying to improve the quality of their family lives.

---

22. Over two-fifths of the current student population are 25 years of age or older. See footnote 3.
23. "Called and Gifted: The American Catholic Laity," in *Pastoral Letters,* vol. 4, 1975-1983, no. 19.

Setting up programs that embody this vision is a concrete way of encouraging others and of demonstrating what can be done with cooperative efforts. The goal of this style of leadership is to multiply the centers of activity and to unleash the creative power of the Spirit so that the community of faith can be an authentic sign and instrument of the kingdom.

25. Some professional campus ministers exercise the universal priesthood based on baptism, and others are ordained priests or deacons through the sacrament of holy orders. It is a sign of hope that a growing number of lay people serve as leaders in the faith community on campus. We commend members of religious orders who continue to make important contributions by gathering and encouraging the faithful. It is of historical significance that women "who in the past have not always been allowed to take their proper role in the Church's ministry"[24] find greater opportunities on campus to exercise their leadership abilities. Deacons often possess special talents and important life experiences that enhance their leadership skills. We encourage the priests who help form the faith community in a great variety of ways. Their prayerful celebration of the Eucharist, which invites active participation and manifests the unity of the congregation, as well as their compassionate celebration of the sacrament of reconciliation are especially important. All those officially appointed to lead the Church on campus have a great responsibility to form vibrant communities of faith and an exciting challenge to bring forth the gifts of individual believers.

26. In order to meet these challenges, campus ministers often form teams which provide a broader base of leadership to the faith community. Individual members bring their unique personalities and gifts to the team and work cooperatively to set direction and carry out some programs. The team members are co-responsible for the well-being of the faith community and accountable in their own areas of activity and competency. At the same time, they have the support of their colleagues when needed. Praying together helps the men and women on the team to keep in mind the true source and goal of their mission and to experience a sense of solidarity. We encourage the formation of such team ministries, which serve as models of ministry and community for the rest of the Church.

27. There are certain general challenges faced by all campus ministers. To be effective, ministers must attend to their own spiritual development. Campus ministers who are serious about their prayer life and can speak openly about their relationship to God will be able to direct others. Ministers who have wrestled with the great questions

---

24. Ibid., no. 27.

of meaning, purpose, and identity can offer helpful guidance to other genuine searchers. Those who have appropriated the faith and mined the riches of the Catholic heritage will be in a better position to invite others to join the faith community. If they genuinely care about the weak and the oppressed, they will inspire others to work for social justice. Finally, campus ministers who have achieved an integration of faith and culture will naturally serve as role models for students and faculty members who are trying to achieve a similar synthesis. In summation, the leaders of the faith community must be perceived as persons who know the struggles of life and who are working to develop themselves spiritually.

28. Campus ministers are also called to empower the faith community and its individual members in the task of helping their colleges or universities to reach their full potential. Ministers who have a genuine respect for academic life and for institutions of higher education will see clearly the importance of this work and find creative ways to respond. A healthy self-confidence will enable them to relate openly with faculty members and administrators and to empathize with students who are struggling with their personal growth. By gaining the respect and confidence of the various members of the academic community, they will find many ways to get involved on campus and promote human values in the institution. Campus ministers with solid training and good credentials will have more opportunities to enter into the mainstream of academic life on campus. Today, it is clear that campus ministers must not remain on the margins of the academic community but must accept the call to bring the light of the Gospel to the very center of that world.

29. To prepare for meeting all these challenges, we encourage campus ministers to take responsibility for their own personal and professional development. Clear contractual arrangements that include carefully defined expectations and procedures for accountability and evaluation help to set a proper framework for their personal enrichment. Membership in appropriate professional organizations, participation in activities on diocesan, regional, and national levels, involvement in support groups with other campus ministers, and regular interaction with a spiritual director can provide motivation and direction for improving their performance. If campus ministers are to remain flexible in response to the rapidly changing needs of the campus community, they need to study contemporary developments in Scripture and theology while deepening their knowledge of the Christian tradition. Attaining an advanced degree or achieving competency in a particular area not only contributes to professional development, but helps gain respect in the academic world. Today, skills in counseling and spiritual direction, as well as knowledge of family systems and life cycles, group dynamics, and adult education are especially valuable for leaders of the faith community. An understanding of the nature and dynamics of the academic world enables campus ministers to apply Christian teachings and values more effectively.

30. In addition to these common challenges, campus ministers find that the unique situations of their particular campuses create their own concerns and opportunities. For example, campus ministers at community colleges must respond to the needs of students who live at home and have jobs. They often need assistance in defining their roles and responsibilities in the home. Many students are married and are present on campus only for their classes. Some ministers have been able, in these situations, to form small faith communities around shared prayer or social action projects. At these two-year colleges, the ministry of presence is especially important, as is securing the support and active involvement of interested faculty members. These institutions are often open to the addition of religious courses into the curriculum. Skills in marriage and career counseling are especially valuable. It is important for these campus ministers to maintain close relationships with neighboring parishes because that is where many students will find their primary faith community.

31. It is possible also to identify other particular challenges. Campus ministers on private denominational campuses must be especially attentive to the ecumenical dimension. Those who work primarily with minority students, including recently arrived immigrants, refugees, and international students, must be in touch with their cultural background and family experiences, as well as the unique challenges they face in the academic world. Large state schools produce logistical problems for campus ministers in handling so many students. On commuter campuses, making contact with students is difficult in itself. All of these particular challenges represent opportunities for creative ministry.

32. Professional campus ministers are crucial to the work of the Church on campus. They bear the heavy responsibility of guiding the faith community and empowering others to assist in the task of helping higher education reach its full potential. The extent and intensity of these demands remind them that they must gather others to assist them. They should expect support and guidance from the diocesan director of campus ministry, who is the usual liaison with the bishop and the local diocese. The director can help facilitate their personal growth, call for a proper accountability, and possible diocesan-wide programming. As the diocesan bishop's representative, the director encourages the interaction among campus ministers in the diocese who serve on public, Catholic, and other private campuses. We recognize our responsibility as bishops to offer all campus ministers moral support, to provide financial assistance to the degree this is needed and possible, and to help them achieve the competency they need to be effective witnesses of the Gospel.

IV. Aspects of Campus Ministry

33. After situating campus ministry in the relationship between the Church and higher education and discussing the persons who perform this service, we now turn our attention to six aspects of campus ministry. These ministerial functions reflect the general mission of the Church on campus and the distinctive situation of higher education today. In her ministry, the faith community on campus must be faithful to the essential teachings of the Church and, at the same time, read the signs of the times and accordingly adapt the message of the Gospel to meet the needs of the academic community.[25]

A. Forming the Faith Community

1. Community and Alienation on Campus

34. Campus ministry attempts to form faith communities in an academic environment that knows both a healthy sense of solidarity and a good deal of alienation. Ideally, colleges and universities gather teachers and students together into a community of shared values and common dedication to the pursuit of truth. In fact, on campuses there is a good deal of collaborative effort. Organizations abound, close friendships are formed, interest groups gather the like-minded. Many administrators, faculty members, and students move easily in this world and find that it satisfies their needs for companionship and involvement. Many Christians freely gather into communities of faith in which they share their strengths and gifts with others.

35. On the other hand, lonely voices on campus cry out for intimacy,

---

25. "The Church in the Modern World," no. 44.

and mildly estranged individuals express a desire for more personal interaction. Students who leave home and come to large universities often feel lost in the vast impersonal world. The world of research and scholarship can seem cold and demeaning to graduate students. Commuter students who are on campus only briefly for classes do not have the opportunity to form close bonds with others. Some sense of alienation seems inevitable for international students who must cope with a new culture. Recently arrived immigrant and refugee students experience the isolation and loneliness of being separated from family and homeland. Older students worry about fitting in and being accepted and, at times, have the added complication of marital and family pressures. Even students in small private colleges can experience a lack of depth in their relationships and a consequent sense of estrangement. Complaints are also heard from faculty members about the superficiality of their relationships with close colleagues and the lack of opportunities for interaction with those in other departments. Some feel cut off from the centers of power, as important academic decisions are made without their input. The difficulty of gathering students for anything except social events and concerts is a continuing problem for student affairs leaders. Administrators speak openly about the fragmentation of campus life and search for ways to overcome it. The voices of estrangement are many and varied. Campus ministers who listen well know that there is a genuine hunger for community in the academic world, as well as a strong sense of solidarity.

2. The Importance of Christian Community

36. The call to form communities of faith flows both from the very nature of the Gospel itself and from the pastoral situation on campus. Christianity is ecclesial by its very nature. The communal character of salvation is already clear in the Hebrew Scriptures: "It has pleased God, however, to make [human beings] holy and save them not merely as individuals without any mutual bonds, but by making them into a single people, a people which acknowledges Him in truth and serves Him in holiness."[26] This truth was exemplified in the life of Jesus Christ who, led by the Spirit, gathered together a community of followers. The Twelve served as official witnesses of his saving mission and symbolic representation of the new people of God. Through his striking parables and miraculous signs he proclaimed the kingdom in which all human beings, animated by the Spirit, were

---

26. "Dogmatic Constitution on the Church," no. 9.

22

to live in peace and harmony. The death and resurrection of Jesus brought a new outpouring of the Spirit which "makes the Church grow, perpetually renews Her and leads Her to perfect union with Her Spouse."[27] Under the influence of the Spirit, the Church remembers the prayer of Jesus that "all may be one, Father, as you are in me and I am in you, so that the world may believe" (Jn 17:21). All the baptized, empowered by the Spirit, share responsibility for forming the Church into a genuine community of worship and service. Guided by the Holy Spirit, the Church is called, with all of its limitations and sinfulness, to wend its way through history as the visible sign of the unity of the whole human family and as an instrument of reconciliation for all.[28]

37. Today, the Church on campus is challenged to be a credible sign of unity and a living reminder of the essential interdependence and solidarity of all people. Thus, the faith community seeks to gather those who wish to serve others and to bring healing to those in the academic world who are restricted by artificial barriers and wounded by alienating practices. The Church gains credibility when the dream of community produces genuine commitment and intelligent effort. In the ideal community of faith, the Mystery that rules over our lives is named and worshipped. Dedication to Christ is fostered, and openness to all truth, goodness, and beauty is maintained. The life of the Spirit is nourished and discussed. Positive images of God, Christ, Mary, and the afterlife warm the heart and structure the imagination. The common good is emphasized and personal development encouraged. Individuals experience true freedom and at the same time accept responsibility for the well-being of the group. Traditional wisdom is available and the best contemporary insights are valued. Prayerful liturgies enable us to praise God with full hearts and create a sense of belonging, as well as nourish people for a life of service. Members are known by name and newcomers are welcomed. Unity of faith is celebrated while legitimate pluralism is recognized. Individuals find both support and challenge and can share their joys and sorrows. The members hunger for justice and have the courage to fight the dehumanizing tendencies in the culture. The community knows the sorrows of life but remains a people of hope. In this ideal community of faith, the members are of one heart and mind (Acts 4:32) and receive the spirit of wisdom which brings them to full knowledge of Jesus Christ who is the head of the Church (Eph 1:17-23).

---

27. Ibid., no. 4.
28. Ibid., no. 48.

38. By working toward the dream of genuine community, campus ministry unleashes human potential and contributes to the common struggle against the forces of alienation. A Church serious about building community reminds others of the beauty and nobility of a life lived in harmony and peace. The baptized who experience acceptance, healing, and empowerment in the faith community are better prepared to bring an understanding ear, a reconciling touch, and an encouraging voice to alienated persons on campus.

3. The Challenge of Forming the Faith Community

39. When the dream of a genuine faith community is alive, then the search for effective strategies is intensified. Attitudes are crucial. Campus ministers whose personal outreach is warm and welcoming are likely to gain the active participation of others in the community. The ministry of presence in which leaders of the faith community make themselves available by being on campus regularly and getting involved in activities and events is a valuable way of making initial contact with potential members of the faith community and of enhancing existing relationships. Administrators, faculty members, and students who sense that they are valued as persons and that their talents and initiatives are appreciated, will find involvement more attractive.
40. On many campuses, Mass and communion services have proven to be powerful means of building community. Ministers who put a great deal of effort into preparing liturgies that are in accord with the Church's liturgical directives and are prayerful, coherent, and aesthetically pleasing, generally find an enthusiastic response. If they keep in mind the sensibilities of the academic community and strive for wide participation, the broad use of legitimate liturgical options, and a flexible style, the inherent community-building power of the Eucharist is enhanced. There is a greater recognition today that stimulating homilies that apply the Gospel realistically and convey positive religious images are especially important in fostering genuine religious conversion and a sense of closeness to the worshipping community and the Church as a whole.[29] It is a sign of hope for the future that so many collegians are gaining a deeper appreciation of the power of the Eucharist to raise the mind and heart to God and to serve as "a sacrament of love, a sign of unity, a bond of charity."[30]
41. In many sacramentally oriented campus ministries, the adult

---

29. Fee et al., *Young Catholics* (New York: William H. Sadlier, Inc., 1980), pp. 154-55.
30. "Constitution on the Sacred Liturgy," in *Documents of Vatican II,* no. 47.

catechumenate process has become an especially valuable means of incorporating new members into the Catholic Church and strengthening the faith of those who are already members. As a result, the Catholic faith community becomes stronger, more attractive, and inviting. The presence of adults who have freely chosen to join the Church moves some members to think more deeply about their own relationships to the Church. Those who serve as sponsors often gain a new appreciation of their faith and a renewed sense of the Church as a community of committed believers. A community will attract newcomers as more and more of its members demonstrate enthusiasm for the faith and an attractive style of Christian living.

42. On other campuses, different forms of community building predominate. For example, campus ministers at some commuter colleges form community through bible study programs. Through personal contact, they gather together faculty members and students for shared reading and discussion of the Scriptures. This leads into group prayer and joint projects to serve others. Such programs reveal the power of the Scriptures to call individuals out of their isolation and to give them a sense of solidarity as they struggle to live out the Christian life in the academic world.

43. The experience of Christian community on campus is important to the life of the whole Church. Students who have such a positive experience and are taught their responsibilities to the larger Church will continue to be a very valuable resource for family, parish, and diocesan life when they leave school. Campus ministers can prepare for this by maintaining good ties with local parishes and giving students the opportunity to be of service there.

44. Building up the community of faith on campus is the responsibility of all baptized persons. The desire to serve and the hunger for community must be tapped. Individuals who are personally invited to join in this task and given freedom and encouragement to use their gifts and talents for the benefit of the community are more likely to respond. It is the duty of leaders to provide vision and encourage others to accept their responsibilities. The task of forming Christian communities on campus encounters great difficulties but also brings deep satisfaction. This crucial aspect of campus ministry is worthy of vigorous and creative efforts so that the Catholic community can be an authentic sign and instrument of the kingdom on campus.

B. Appropriating the Faith

1. The Challenges to Faith on Campus

45. Campus ministry has the task of enabling Catholics to achieve a more adult appropriation of their faith so that they can live in greater communion with God and the Church, give more effective witness to the Gospel, and face the challenges to belief that exist in the academic world. In the classroom, students learn to question traditional assumptions and to tolerate diverse opinions on important questions that cause some to doubt their religious beliefs. Most students eventually encounter the modern critics of religion who charge that belief is either infantile or dehumanizing. In some classes, the scientific method that has advanced human learning so effectively is presented as a total world view, which supplants religion and renders obsolete other approaches to truth. Some professors give the impression that maturation involves rejection of religious beliefs. In these and other ways, the academic world challenges the traditional belief systems of many students.

46. Campus life tends to reinforce these intellectual challenges. Catholic students, at times, find their faith shaken by encountering peers who profess widely divergent world views and life styles. Today, a significant number of Catholics are attracted away from their religious heritage by fundamentalist groups that employ aggressive proselytizing tactics and promise clear answers and instant security in the midst of a frightening and complex world. When students learn more about the harsh realities of life and the monstrous evils that have been part of human history, they are, at times, forced to question their belief in a God who seems callous in allowing such human suffering. Finally, the whirl of campus life, with its exhilarating freedom and the pressure of making good grades, can so dominate the attention of students that they drift away from their faith without much real thought.

47. Many Catholics on campus, including faculty members, are unprepared to deal with intellectual challenges to the faith. They are unable to explain their belief to interested friends or to defend it against attacks by hostile critics. Their understanding of the faith has not kept pace with their knowledge in other areas. The legitimate pluralism of theology and spirituality in the Church confuses them. They have not achieved an adult appropriation of their religion that would enable them to speak about it not only with conviction but also with intelligence. At times, this produces frustration and anger over the inadequacy of their religious training.

48. These problems are intensified by the general religious illiteracy in our culture. Public education is not committed to passing on the religious heritage. Many good people do not recognize the importance of religious knowledge for a well-rounded education. Most colleges and universities still do not have departments or programs of religious studies, nor do they provide adequate opportunities to explore the religious dimension of various disciplines in the curriculum. In the academic world, there are still those who think that teaching about religion necessarily involves proselytizing and that it cannot be done in an academically sound way. This attitude compounds the problems of campus ministers who seek to promote a more mature appropriation of the faith among Catholics.

49. On the positive side, the challenges on campus prompt some Catholics to explore and deepen their belief. Doubts, which are frequently a part of faith development, at times lead to further study and renewed convictions. The academic world provides intellectual stimulation and helpful resources for those who want to explore their religious tradition. There is a growing interest in religious studies and an increase in programs and courses around the country. Some public institutions have excellent departments or programs in religious studies that demonstrate that this can be done legally and according to proper academic standards. Today, within the academic community a few voices are heard insisting that a well-educated person should have a knowledge of religion. At some institutions, campus ministry has produced excellent programs in theological studies that supplement the offerings in the curriculum through a wide variety of credit and noncredit courses, seminars, and lectures. The faculty members and students who have achieved a more mature appropriation of their faith provide important witness on campus and are a sign of hope in the struggle against religious illiteracy.

2. Principles for Appropriating the Faith

50. By its very nature, Christianity calls us to an ever-deeper understanding and appreciation of our faith. Baptism initiates us into a lifelong process in which we are gradually formed anew in the image of our Creator and thus grow in knowledge (Col 3:10). The Scriptures remind us that this process means moving beyond childish ways to more mature approaches: "Let us, then, be children no longer, tossed here and there, carried about by every wind of doctrine that originates in human trickery and skill in proposing error. Rather, let us profess the truth in love and grow to the full maturity of Christ the head" (Eph 4:14-16). The Scriptures also call us to move beyond illusion to a deeper way of thinking and relating to God: "You must lay aside your former way of life and the old self which deteriorates through illusion and desire, and acquire a fresh, spiritual way of thinking" (Eph 4:22-23). Members of the faith community who achieve a more mature grasp of their Christian faith are in a better position to understand themselves and their world. Those who continue their theological education are better able to reflect on their experiences in the light of the Gospel. By assimilating the meanings and values in the Christian tradition, believers are better equipped to affirm the positive meanings and values in the culture and to resist those who are opposed to the Gospel. Individuals who are well grounded in their own Catholic heritage are better prepared to enter into ecumenical and interfaith dialogue and cooperation. The Second Vatican Council reminded us that Christians have the task of achieving "a public, persistent, and universal presence in the whole enterprise of advancing higher culture."[31] The Council called upon Christians to "shoulder society's heavier burdens and to witness the faith to the world."[32] Those best qualified for this great work are the believers who have understood the implications of their faith and are able to articulate their deepest beliefs. The Scriptures offer us this advice: "Should anyone ask you the reason for this hope of yours, be ever ready to reply, but speak gently and respectfully" (1 Pt 3:15-16). To respond credibly, intelligently, and sensitively to honest inquiry requires careful and systematic preparation. All the members of the community of faith have a right to the kind of theological education that prepares them to meet this responsibility.[33] When we consider the demands of the academic world, it is clear that the Church on campus has a special responsibility to enable all of its members to appropriate the faith more deeply in order to give effective witness to the academic community.

51. The importance of achieving an intelligent appropriation of the faith can also be established by examining the nature and purpose of education. As we have noted elsewhere, "a truly liberating and elevating education is incomplete without the study of theology or religion."[34] We must continue to encourage the study of religion in our society as a whole because, as Cardinal Newman insisted, religious truth has an inherent value and is "not only a portion but a

---

31. "Declaration on Christian Education," no. 10.
32. Ibid.
33. Ibid., no. 2.
34. "Catholic Higher Education," no. 22. In this regard, it is important to distinguish theology, which involves a faith perspective and commitment, from religious studies, which can proceed in a more neutral fashion.

condition of general knowledge."[35] Educated persons should know something of the history, teachings, and practices of the various world religions and be especially versed in the Judeo-Christian tradition, which shaped Western civilization in general and our own culture in particular. Furthermore, they should be aware of the religious aspects of other disciplines, such as literature, history, and art, as well as the religious dimension of our contemporary culture.[36]

52. Traditionally, theology has been known to the Church as the "Queen of the Sciences." Today, we must emphasize its continuing power to keep alive the great questions of meaning, purpose, and identity and to provide a coherent vision of life, which serves as a framework and unifying principle for all learning. Theological study helps to produce the kind of intellect described by Cardinal Newman "which cannot be partial, cannot be exclusive, cannot be impetuous, cannot be at a loss, cannot but be patient, collected, and majestically calm, because it discerns the end in every delay; because it ever knows where it stands, and how its path lies from one point to another."[37] The study of theology not only helps us gain this kind of perspective, but also helps us to understand in greater depth Jesus Christ who reveals to us the secrets of the Father. In a well-rounded Christian education, the teachings of the Church are presented with fidelity to the magisterium and with the contemporary situation in mind. This kind of solid theological training enables the members of the faith community to achieve a genuine synthesis of their rich religious heritage and the best in the contemporary culture.

53. A Christian faith that fails to seek a more mature understanding is not faithful to its own inner dynamism. A culture that is unaware of its religious roots and substance is impoverished and weakened. Educated Christians who have not grown beyond an adolescent level of faith development are limited in their ability to achieve personal integration and to make a contribution to society. These dangers remind campus ministry to maintain its dedication to forming the best possible learning community. The goal is that all of the members of the community achieve a deep understanding of their faith so that they are better prepared to witness to the kingdom of truth in the world.

---

35. John Henry Cardinal Newman, *The Idea of a University* (Garden City, N.Y.: Image Books, 1959), p. 103.

36. "Catholic Higher Education," no. 22.

37. Newman, *The Idea of a University*, p. 159.

3. Strategies for Appropriating the Faith

54. In order to move toward these goals, it is vital that campus ministry creates a climate in which theological learning is respected. Campus ministers help to produce this climate by reminding all the members that they need an adult appropriation of the faith that matches their learning in other areas, in order to function as effective Christians in the world. This message is strengthened if the campus ministers are perceived as being serious about continuing their own theological education. The presence of faculty members and students who are already finding enlightenment and satisfaction in theological studies is a powerful motivation for others. A tradition of pursuing theological learning must be established in which all the members sense their responsibility to achieve a more mature understanding of their faith.

55. If the faith community shares this broad appreciation of the importance of religious studies, then individual programs are more likely to be successful. Program planners should be aware of the courses on campus that deal with religious matters, as well as the current needs and interests of faculty and students. For example, the existence on campus of an increasing number of fundamentalist groups has intensified the need for scripture courses that combine the historical-critical method with opportunities for personal application and shared prayer. Such courses tap the current interest in relating the Scriptures to everyday life and prepare members of the faith community to deal with the aggressive recruiting methods employed by some fundamentalist groups. In general, campus ministry should supplement the religious offerings in the curriculum and provide a wide variety of opportunities for Catholics to study and appropriate their religious heritage and to reflect critically on their experiences in the light of the Gospel.

56. Effective strategies must deal realistically with the situations of the targeted audiences. Theological studies can be made more attractive for students by arranging credit for courses offered by the campus ministry program. For example, through a theologian-in-residence program, students on a state university campus could gain academic credit from a nearby Catholic college for theology courses taught at the campus ministry center on the state campus. Programs for faculty members and administrators must respect their vast experience while, at the same time, taking into account their general lack of systematic theological training.

57. Campus ministry has the responsibility not only to provide theological education for Catholics, but also to work with others to improve the response of higher education to the problem of religious illiteracy in our culture. The key to making progress in this area is to overcome the unfortunate assumption that the study of religion cannot be a genuine academic discipline. The academic community must be shown that religion is worthy of careful and systematic study because it is central to human existence and is an important well-spring of our culture. Professors who deal with religious questions in their courses can help to overcome this bias by teaching this material according to rigorous academic standards of objectivity and with obvious respect for opposing opinions. If the bias against religion as an academic subject can be overcome, then a variety of positive steps might be possible, such as establishing a religious studies program, organizing a lectureship devoted to religious questions, and founding an endowed chair for Catholic thought. If the climate on campus were more open, then campus ministers with advanced degrees might find opportunities to teach part time in appropriate departments or programs. Even if some of these larger initiatives are not possible, campus ministers still can provide a valuable service for students by identifying the courses on campus in which the religious aspect is treated well and fairly.

58. In the faith community, it is understood that religious literacy is for the well-being of society and that theological learning is for the sake of a deepened faith. The goal is an adult appropriation of the faith that fosters personal commitment to Christ and encourages intelligent witness in the world on behalf of the Gospel.

C. Forming the Christian Conscience

1. Moral Relativism on Campus

59. The Church on campus must facilitate the formation of a Christian conscience in its members so that they can make decisions based on gospel values and, thereby, resist moral relativism. Many questions of personal values and ethics inevitably arise for individuals in the academic community. Students are concerned with the moral dimension of such matters as relating to family members, abortion, sexual conduct, drinking and drugs, forming friendships, honesty in their studies, and pursuing a career. At times, faculty members experience a conflict of values as they try to balance their research and teaching and attempt to remain objective in the classroom while expressing their personal opinions. Their integrity can be tested as they fight against grade inflation and struggle to maintain academic freedom while accepting external funding for research. Individual courses often produce particular ethical and value questions. This occurs in obvious ways in philosophy, literature, and the life sciences and in more subtle ways in the physical sciences and technology courses. For example, a computer course may be based on assumptions about human nature that need to be discussed. Ethical questions also arise in relation to institutional policies and practices, such as whether a particular college or university is demonstrating a proper respect and care for the athletes it recruits and utilizes.

60. As members of the academic community deal with these questions, they unavoidably come under the influence of the moral climate that dominates their particular college or university. The eyes of faith discern, in the academic world as a whole, the predictable mixture of grace and sin that characterizes all institutions. On the one hand, the climate is shaped by high idealism, dedicated service, a long tradition of civil discourse, great tolerance for opposing views, sensitive care for individuals, hard work, and a deep love for freedom. Examples of personal virtue are evident in students who resist intense peer pressure and maintain their high moral standards; in faculty members who make financial sacrifices to stay in the academic world and who carry on their teaching and research with responsibility and integrity; in administrators who consistently speak the truth and treat all members of the academic community humanely. Organizations and groups often help raise the moral tone of the campus by being involved in charitable activities and espousing high ideals. In some fields, such as business, medicine, law, and the life sciences, more courses are being offered that deal with ethical questions. Periodically, a wave of idealism sweeps our campuses which reminds us of the great potential for goodness in the academic community.

61. On the other hand, Christians recognize in the academic world a strong strain of moral relativism that tends to reduce genuine freedom to license and an open-minded tolerance to mindlessness. Rational discourse about ethical questions degenerates into nothing more than sharing personal feelings. Sin is reduced to neurosis or blamed on societal pressures. The project of forming a healthy conscience is neglected in favor of a selfish individualism. In this climate, some persons assume that it is impossible or useless to make judgments about whether particular actions are right or wrong, whether some values are better than others, and whether certain patterns of behavior are constructive or destructive.

62. If this philosophy predominates on campus, Catholics are hard pressed to maintain their values and principles. They find it harder to mount an effective critique of institutional practices that violate the high ideals of higher education and fail to respect the dignity of human beings. Young adults who are moving through various stages of moral development are often confused by mixed messages and conflicting philosophies. Students must contend with peer pressures to enter into the drug scene, to cheat on exams, to engage in promiscuous sexual activity, to have abortions, and, in general, to adopt a hedonistic life style. Some older students find that their commitments to spouses and families are called into question. Faculty members and administrators, at times, experience subtle pressures to go along with morally questionable institutional policies and practices.

2. Conscience in a Catholic Perspective

63. In this situation, campus ministry has the crucial task of assisting in the formation of Catholic consciences so that individuals who will continue to face very complex ethical issues throughout their lives are prepared to make good moral judgments according to gospel values. The Scriptures remind us: "Do not conform yourself to this age but be transformed by the renewal of your mind so that you may judge what is God's will, what is good, pleasing and perfect" (Rom 12:2). Conscience formation involves just such a transforming renewal of mind in accord with the will of God.[38] For, conscience is that "most secret core and sanctuary of a person where one is close with God."[39] There we hear the voice of God echoing in the depths of our being and calling us to heed the law written on our hearts. As Cardinal Newman wrote in the last century: "Conscience does not repose on itself, but vaguely reaches forward to something beyond itself and dimly discerns a sanction higher than self for its decisions, as is evidenced in that keen sense of obligation and responsibility which informs them."[40] "Conscience, then, though it is inviolable, is not a law unto itself."[41] It is rather through our conscience that we detect a call from God, summoning us to love the good and avoid evil. It is in response to this call, heard in the secret recesses of our hearts, that we make the judgments of conscience required by the concrete circumstances of our daily lives. This requires an informed conscience, one nourished in prayer, enlightened by study, structured by the Gospel, and guided by the teachings of the Church. Self-deception is all too easy; blindness and illusion can easily mislead

---

38. "The Church in the Modern World," no. 16.
39. Ibid.
40. Cited in "The Church in Our Day," in *Pastoral Letters,* vol. 3, 1962-1974, no. 205.
41. Ibid., no. 206.

us. "Beloved, do not trust every spirit, but put the spirits to a test to see if they belong to God" (1 Jn 4:1). Thus, we need the community of faith to challenge our illusions and to call us to greater self-honesty.

64. In emphasizing the objective call from God, mediated through the Church, we do not want to lose sight of the fact that the divine summons must be answered freely and intelligently. "Morality, then, is not simply something imposed on us from without, but is ingrained in our being; it is the way we accept our humanity as restored to us in Christ."[42] Thus, all human beings are bound to follow their conscience faithfully in order that they may set the course of their lives directly toward God.[43] We are freely responsible for ourselves and cannot shift that burden to anyone else. We come to the full measure of freedom by putting on the mind of Christ. When Christ freed us, he meant us to remain free (Gal 5:1). By preaching Christ and his message of freedom, the community of faith seeks to inform the consciences of all of its members. The Christian who possesses a conscience structured by the Gospel of Christ and who is guided by the continuing presence of Christ's spirit in the Church is better prepared to deal with the rapidly changing complexities of the world today. When genuine virtue is acquired, then good actions flow more spontaneously and new strength is found to live according to one's ideals. Individuals whose conscience has been tutored by the Gospel understand that their task is not only to resist evil but to help transform the world.

65. This portrayal of the informed Christian conscience stands in stark contrast to moral relativism. If morality is based on the call of God, then it cannot be totally arbitrary. Moral relativism betrays the essential structure of human persons who are ultimately dependent on a God who calls all of us to account. A conscience that remembers its source and is nourished and supported by the community of faith is the best resource for dealing with the complex questions of personal values and ethics.

3. Methods of Conscience Formation

66. Campus ministry is called to bring the Gospel of Christ to bear on the moral problems faced by members of the academic community. This can be done by personal encounters such as spiritual direction and counseling, as well as through homilies, classes, and seminars. When campus ministers address these questions, it is vital

---

42. "To Live in Christ Jesus," in *Pastoral Letters,* vol. 4, 1975-1983, no. 22.
43. "Declaration on Religious Freedom," in *Documents of Vatican II,* no. 3.

that they are perceived as being in touch with the texture and complexities of the moral problems generated by campus life. They also must have a working knowledge of the wisdom found in the Catholic tradition on particular moral questions. A good way for campus ministers to multiply their effectiveness is by facilitating peer ministry programs in which individuals who have successfully dealt with particular moral problems can help others in similar situations. For example, a senior athlete who managed to keep a healthy perspective on sports and maintain good grades could be prepared to speak with other athletes struggling to keep their values intact in highly pressurized situations. Students who have freed themselves from the drug scene could help others interested in breaking their drug habits. For older students struggling to keep their marriages together, conversations with faculty members who kept their commitments in similar circumstances could be mutually beneficial in enriching their married lives. In all such peer ministry approaches, it is important that those serving others are well prepared through a proper grounding in gospel ideals and church teachings on these moral questions. Engaging members of the faith community in such peer ministry programs is a valuable way of extending the effort to form Christian consciences.

67. Courses or seminars provide a more structured approach to the formation of conscience. For example, undergraduate students can be gathered for a seminar on the question of premarital sex, contraception, and abortion. An open atmosphere is needed so that the students can speak freely about the prevailing attitudes and peer pressures on campus, as well as about their own outlooks and modes of decision making. A skillful leader can use the discussion as a basis for bringing out the Christian teaching that insists that sexuality is best understood in terms of personal relationships and that intercourse is a sign of the total commitment associated with marriage. In dealing with this and all areas of personal morality, the Catholic tradition must be presented as containing a wisdom that illuminates the mystery of human existence and encourages behavior that is in the best interest of the individual and society.

68. A good deal of conscience formation must be done on an individual basis. Counseling, spiritual direction, and the celebration of the sacrament of reconciliation provide excellent opportunities to apply Christian teachings to an individual's precise situation and current stage of moral development. Through these means, persons can gradually discover the illusions and destructive patterns that impede the development of a conscience fully attuned to the Gospel. Such settings also provide the occasion to proclaim the great mercy of our God, who deals patiently with our weaknesses and guides us gradually to full growth in Christ.

69. If campus ministry hopes to deal effectively with questions of personal values and ethics, it must be concerned with the general moral climate on campus. When individuals maintain high moral standards despite pressures, they make an important personal contribution to the moral tone of the academic community. Since colleges and universities have the task of fostering critical thinking and transmitting our cultural heritage, they should include questions of values and ethics in this general mission. Members of the faith community who understand the importance of the moral dimension of life are called to join with others in promoting a more extensive and informed discussion of ethical issues on campus. This can be done in a great variety of ways, such as facilitating an appreciation of the need for courses on ethics in each department and program, encouraging professors to treat the questions of ethics and values that arise in their courses, and sponsoring lectures and seminars on particular moral questions. It is especially helpful to get the whole academic community involved in concentrated discussions. For example, campus ministers could join with other interested groups in sponsoring a "Values and Ethics Week" on campus, designed to deal directly with moral issues. During this week, all professors are encouraged to spend class time discussing the ethical implications of their courses. Informal discussions and structured seminars are arranged throughout the week. In order to give the whole program momentum and status, major speakers are brought in to address current ethical concerns. The important element in these strategies is to move the academic community to carry on its proper task of promoting critical thinking in the area of values and ethics.

D. Educating for Justice

1. The Search for Justice on Campus

70. Campus ministry is called to make the struggle for social justice an integral part of its mission. The academic world generates questions not only of personal morality but also of social justice, which includes issues of peace and war, as well as reverence for life in all phases of its development. Some questions arise as colleges and universities determine their internal policies and practices. How, for instance, should they balance their concern for quality education with a policy of open access that gives disadvantaged students the opportunity for higher education?[44] Issues also emerge as higher education interacts with other institutions. A prime example is whether universities can maintain their integrity, freedom, and a balanced research program while accepting massive funding from the Department of Defense for research on weapons systems. Periodically, a social justice issue captures the imagination of a significant number of students on campus, producing demonstrations and an appeal for direct action. A more sustained commitment to particular justice issues is demonstrated by some individuals, such as those who remain active in the peace movement over a long period of time and those who maintain the effort to gain legal protection for unborn human life. Such persons of conscience often encounter apathy, misunderstanding, and rejection and therefore deserve the special support and encouragement of the Church.

71. The academic community could generate intense debate over all these issues. In general terms, some want the university to remain detached from social issues, while others look for more active involvement to achieve a more just society. Most agree that higher education makes a valuable contribution by providing a forum for discussing the great questions of the day in a civil and reasoned fashion so that constructive solutions can be worked out.

72. Finally, it must be admitted that there is a great deal of apathy in evidence on campus today. Many are caught up in their own concerns and have little if any interest in social matters. Others who have been actively involved are now weary of the battles and have retreated into less demanding activities. Most students do not even think in terms of altering unjust structures through political action or social involvement. In general, alongside striking examples of personal commitment to justice, we sense a strong current of individualism that undercuts concern for the common good and eclipses the urgency of social concerns.

2. Principles of Catholic Social Teaching

73. Campus ministry is called to be a consistent and vigorous advocate for justice, peace, and the reverence for all life. All the baptized should understand that "action on behalf of justice is a significant criterion of the Church's fidelity to its missions. It is not optional, nor is it the work of only a few in the Church. It is something to

---

44. See the report by the Southern Regional Education Board's Commission for Educational Quality, "Access to Quality Undergraduate Education," *Chronicle of Higher Education,* July 3, 1985, p. 9 ff.

which all Christians are called according to their vocations, talents, and situations in life."[45] With this in mind, campus ministers have the responsibility of keeping alive the vision of the Church on campus as a genuine servant community that is dedicated to the works of justice, peace, and reverence for life, in all stages of its development.

74. As we noted in our pastoral letter on peace, "at the center of all Catholic social teaching are the transcendence of God and the dignity of the human person. The human person is the clearest reflection of God's presence in the world; all of the Church's work in pursuit of both justice and peace is designed to protect and promote the dignity of every person. For each person not only reflects God but is the expression of God's creative work and the meaning of Christ's redemptive ministry."[46] In our day, the sanctity of the life of the unborn calls everyone to protect vigorously the life of the most defenseless among us. When we reflect further upon Christ's redemptive ministry, we see that he demonstrated a special care for the poor and the outcasts of his society. He came "to bring glad tidings to the poor, to proclaim liberty to the captives" (Lk 4:18). In identifying himself with suffering persons, he provided us with the strongest motivation to work for justice for all (Mt 25:31-46). In word and deed, Jesus taught us the essential unity between love of God and love of neighbor. His followers understood that if you claim to love God and hate your neighbor, you are a liar (1 Jn 4:20). The Gospel he proclaimed and the Spirit he sent were to transform and renew all of human existence, the social and institutional dimensions, as well as the personal.[47] This analysis suggests a rationale for the commitment to justice, a rationale that should be known and understood by all members of the Church.

75. In the struggle for justice, we need Christians who understand that "knowledge of economics and politics will not in itself bring about justice, unless it is activated by human and religious ideals. However, religious ideals without the necessary secular expertise will not provide the kind of leadership needed to influence our complex society."[48] The faith community on campus, which includes individuals with significant academic achievements, is especially well equipped to achieve the integration of an informed faith with knowl-

---

45. United States Catholic Conference, *Sharing the Light of Faith: National Catechetical Directory for Catholics of the United States* (Washington, D.C.: USCC Office of Publishing and Promotion Services, 1979), no. 160.
46. "The Challenge of Peace: God's Promise and Our Response," in *Pastoral Letters*, vol. 4, 1975-1983, no. 15.
47. "The Church in the Modern World," no. 26.
48. "Catholic Higher Education," no. 39.

edge and skill in the social arena. To accomplish this, there must be great emphasis on "teaching and learning the tradition of Catholic social thought, the creation of an environment for learning that reflects a commitment to justice, and an openness on the part of all Catholics to change personal attitudes and behavior."[49] We call special attention to the coherent body of Catholic social thought developed during the past century in papal encyclicals and reflected in our pastoral letters.[50] It is especially important for Catholics on campus to assimilate these teachings and to use them in their work for justice.

76. As the faith community carries on this educational task, it must remember that the goal is not learning alone, but constructive action to eradicate injustice and to transform society. Christians must learn how to empower individuals and groups to take charge of their own lives and to shape their own destinies. The sin that infects the social order must be not merely analyzed, but attacked. Unjust structures and institutions must be changed, as must policies and laws that fail to respect human life. To be a credible partner in this task, the Church on campus should remember that "any group which ventures to speak to others about justice should itself be just, and should be seen as such. It must therefore submit its own policies, programs, and manner of life to continuing review."[51]

3. Working for Justice

77. Considering the apathy on campus, the faith community has the vital task of raising consciousness on social issues and providing motivation for study and action. Leaders in the faith community who are already actively committed to the struggle for justice are a valuable resource in this effort. Drawing on their own experience, they can try to recruit others to work on specific justice issues. The very presence in the faith community of a core group dedicated to justice serves as an example and invitation to others to contribute their own talents and gifts to create a more humane society. Since apathy and

---

49. "To Do the Work of Justice," in *Pastoral Letters,* vol. 4, 1975-1983, no. 8.
50. For important papal documents, see David J. O'Brien and Thomas A. Shannon, eds., *Renewing the Earth: Catholic Documents of Peace, Justice, and Liberation* (Garden City, N.Y.: Doubleday, 1977). Among our more recent pastoral letters and statements on social justice and peace we call attention to: "The Challenge of Peace: God's Promise and Our Response"; "Brothers and Sisters to Us"; "To Do the Work of Justice"; and our forthcoming pastoral letter on the economy. Finally we note the valuable insights in the pastoral letter *What We Have Seen and Heard: A Pastoral Letter on Evangelization from the Black Bishops of the United States* (Cincinnati: St. Anthony Messenger Press, 1984).
51. *Sharing the Light of Faith,* no. 160.

excessive individualism are such pervasive problems, it is important for all those who are concerned about social justice to sustain their efforts even in the midst of limited successes.

78. Education for justice can be carried out in a variety of ways, ranging from scripture studies and liturgies with a justice orientation to seminars and guided readings on a particular justice issue. Education for justice is enhanced by including an action component. For example, a seminar on hunger that raises consciousness on the issue should include suggested actions, such as joining an appropriate organization, writing congresspersons, or helping out in a local food distribution center. Given the gravity of the nuclear threat, it is especially important to study the issue of peace and war. Such studies should include a discussion of ways to implement the summons to peacemaking contained in our pastoral letter *The Challenge of Peace: God's Promise and Our Response.*

79. Since the struggle for social justice demands involvement and not simply objective analysis, the Church on campus should provide ample opportunities for all of its members to work directly in programs and projects designed to create a more just social order in which peace and reverence for life are possible. Students who are involved in service projects, such as visiting nursing homes, tutoring disadvantaged children, or helping out during vacations in impoverished areas of the country, often grow in appreciation of the people they serve, as well as discover more about the complexity of institutional problems. Systematic reflection on such experiences in the light of the Gospel and the social teachings of the Church enhances their learning and prepares them to be lifelong seekers after justice.

80. Campus ministry has the responsibility to work with others to enable higher education to live up to its commitments and ideals in the area of social justice. Individuals have many opportunities to speak on behalf of those who are powerless. For instance, administrators and faculty members who are helping to set admissions policies or who are involved in hiring decisions can raise up the concerns of the disadvantaged and underrepresented. Students in various organizations can be vigilant so that the rights and sensibilities of international and minority students are respected. Individuals and groups who are attuned to the social dimension of the Gospel can raise ethical questions about institutional policies.

81. Periodically, issues arise that call for a more public response by the Church on campus. Campus ministers, for instance, may be asked to be advocates for a group of students who are seeking redress of legitimate grievances or to provide leadership on a particular issue, such as combating the problems of racism and sexism. These are important opportunities, and campus ministers should respond by drawing on the social teaching of the Church and giving public witness to the Church's concern for justice and peace.

82. Finally, the faith community can touch the conscience of the academic world by sponsoring programs on campus designed to raise consciousness and to promote justice and peace. For example, the Church could organize a day of fasting on campus, with the meal money saved going to help feed hungry people. This is a means of alerting individuals to the magnitude of the problem, of offering concrete help to the hungry, and of witnessing to the social dimension of the Gospel.

E. Facilitating Personal Development

1. Self-fulfillment in the Academic World

83. Campus ministry has the task of promoting the full personal development of the members of the academic community in a setting that is filled with rich, if often neglected, resources for self-fulfillment. Colleges and universities provide marvelous opportunities for healthy personal growth. Classes, lectures, and seminars provide intellectual stimulation. Cultural and social events broaden horizons and facilitate emotional growth. The greatest catalyst for development comes from interaction with the concerned people who make up the academic community. There are campus ministers who can provide guidance for the spiritual quest; administrators who possess broad visions and sensitive hearts; faculty members who are generous in sharing the results of their scholarship; international students who bring the richness of different cultures; and peers who are willing to share friendship and the common struggle for greater maturity. With all of these resources, many individuals find the academic world to be an ideal setting for establishing their identities, forming relationships, developing their talents, preparing for leadership, discerning their vocations, and charting the direction of their lives.

84. On the other hand, this vast potential for growth is often ignored or impeded. Some students think of college only in terms of opening the door to a good job and a secure future. They attend classes, gain credits, and manage to graduate. Learning to think critically and achieving a well-rounded personality through involvement on campus are not part of their program. For these students, the call to self-fulfillment either falls on deaf ears or is interpreted exclusively in terms of a lucrative career and material success. The great potential of higher education to promote personal development can also lie dormant because of the policies and practices of colleges and universities themselves. The traditional task of producing well-rounded individuals who are prepared to serve the common good can recede into the background, as policy decisions are made on the basis of declining enrollments and financial pressures. Recently, voices from within the academic community have been raised, claiming that higher education has not remained faithful to its traditional goals and is not living up to its potential. Some say this is because students are not involved enough in the whole learning process.[52] One report claims that administrators and faculty have lost their nerve in the face of cultural trends and student pressures. It charges that leaders, by failing to insist on the systematic study of the humanities, have effectively deprived students of the cultural heritage that is needed for a well-rounded education.[53] Others decry the lack of a coherent curriculum and call for diverse learning experiences that foster critical thinking and help produce integrated persons who can live responsibly and joyfully as individuals and democratic citizens.[54] Among the critics, there is general agreement that reform is needed so that colleges and universities can achieve their proper goal of facilitating the full personal development of students.

2. Christian Perspectives on Self-fulfillment

85. The Church has the task of distinguishing and evaluating the many voices of our age.[55] Campus ministry must be attuned to the voices of reform in the academic community and be prepared to function as the friend of genuine personal development and as an ally in the quest for healthy self-fulfillment. Our Scriptures remind us that the Spirit calls us to put aside childish ways and to live with greater maturity (1 Cor 14:20). For us Christians, Jesus Christ is the perfectly fulfilled human being.[56] In him, we see the depth of our potential and sublime character of our call. "He blazed a trail, and if we follow it, life and death are made holy and take on a new meaning."[57] By following this path of truth and love, we can grow to full maturity in Christ (Eph 4:15). The Spirit of Jesus, poured out through his death and resurrection, energizes us for the task of

---

52. See "Involvement in Learning."
53. See Bennett, "To Reclaim a Legacy."
54. See "Integrity in the College Curriculum."
55. "The Church in the Modern World.", no. 44.
56. Ibid., no. 22.
57. Ibid.

developing our potential. The same Spirit enables us to recognize and overcome the selfishness in our hearts and the contradictions in the culture that distort the quest for healthy self-fulfillment. When individuals pursue personal development within the community of faith, they are constantly challenged to use their talents in the service of others and to stay open to the Spirit, who accomplishes surprising things in us (Jn 3:8).

86. The Second Vatican Council has given contemporary expression to these biblical insights.[58] Human dignity demands that persons act according to intelligent decisions that are motivated from within. We should pursue our goals in a free choice of what is good and find apt means to achieve these laudable goals. The Christian vision of human existence safeguards the ideal of full human development by rooting it in the sacredness of the person. All persons are worthy of respect and dignity and are called to perfection because they are "a living image of God"[59] and possess a "godlike seed" that has been sown in them.[60] This intrinsic relationship with God, far from limiting the drive for personal development, frees human beings to pursue their fulfillment and happiness with confidence.[61] Furthermore, life in community teaches us that personal freedom acquires new strength when it consents to the requirements of social life, takes on the demands of human partnership, and commits itself to the service of the human family.[62]

87. These principles remind us that Christians must proclaim an ideal of self-fulfillment that is solidly rooted in the sacredness of persons, is placed in the service of the common good, and stays open to the God who is the source of all growth.

88. When campus ministry brings the light of the Gospel to the educational process, the search for personal development leads to a Christian humanism that fuses the positive values and meanings in the culture with the light of faith.[63] Genuine Christian humanists know that the heart is restless until it rests in God and that all persons are unsolved puzzles to themselves, always awaiting the full revelation of God.[64] Thus, for them, personal development is perceived as a

---

58. Ibid., no. 17.

59. "Pastoral Letter on Marxist Communism," in *Pastoral Letters*, vol. 4, 1975-1983, no. 14.

60. "The Church in the Modern World," no. 3.

61. Ibid., no. 21.

62. Ibid., no. 31.

63. This term, *Christian humanism,* has been used in the Church to suggest the ideal of integrating positive cultural values and meanings in a faith perspective. For a recent usage of this term, see "Catholic Higher Education," no. 19.

64. "The Church in the Modern World," no. 21.

lifelong adventure, completed only in the final fulfilling union with the Lord. Christian humanists know that history and all cultures are a mysterious mix of grace and sin[65] and that where sin exists, there grace more abounds (Rom 5:20). Thus, while rejecting the sinful elements in the culture, they are able to assimilate the grace-inspired meanings and values in the world into a comprehensive and organic framework, built on faith in Jesus Christ. As individuals pursue their personal development, the ideal of Christian humanism lights the path and sets the direction.

3. Achieving Personal Development in a Christian Context

89. Campus ministry can facilitate personal development through vibrant sacramental life, courses, seminars, and retreats that enable Catholics on campus to integrate their collegiate experience with their Christian faith. Through pastoral counseling and spiritual direction, campus ministers can encourage individuals to make use of the resources on campus and guide them on the path toward a Christian humanism. This important work is enhanced when the ministers are perceived as persons of prayer who are serious about their own personal growth.

90. It is helpful to multiply these efforts by bringing together, in a personal encounter, those who share the journey toward Christian maturity. A program that enables an individual faculty member to meet on a regular basis outside the classroom with a particular student for friendly conversation and serious discussion provides great opportunities for the kind of exchange that is mutually enriching. Faculty members who are inspired by gospel ideals and undergo training for this kind of program are in an excellent position to be role models for students and, perhaps, spiritual mentors. Students, in turn, bring to the relationship their distinctive experience and challenging questions, which can be a catalyst for mutual growth. A great variety of such programs is possible. The key is to increase the opportunities for more personal contact between members of the faith community so that they can assist one another in the quest for a genuine Christian humanism.

91. Since there is a temptation to reduce self-fulfillment to a selfish individualism, campus ministry provides a valuable service by keeping alive the ideal of Christian humanism, which recognizes that personal growth must be open to the transcendent and in service to the common good. Through prayer groups and liturgical celebrations

---

65. Ibid.

that link life and worship, in lectures and seminars that relate current questions and the Christian tradition, by service projects and actions for justice that put personal gifts at the service of others, the community of faith publicly manifests the Christian ideal of self-fulfillment. The sacrament of reconciliation is a powerful means for personal development since it enables individuals to confront the sins and destructive patterns that inhibit their progress and to hear again the compassionate summons to grow into greater maturity in Christ. Communal penance services that encourage an examination of the distinctive challenges and opportunities for personal development presented by campus life are especially effective in making the ideal of Christian humanism more concrete.

92. Inspired by this ideal, individual members of the faith community have the responsibility to assist their colleges or universities in the task of educating whole persons for lifelong growth and responsible citizenship. This is done in obvious ways by students who study hard and take advantage of cultural opportunities on campus and by faculty members who teach well and take a personal interest in students. In addition, there is the challenge of establishing institutional policies and practices that better facilitate these goals. Today, there is a general consensus that undergraduate education must be improved by various means, such as setting higher standards for classroom work, establishing a more coherent curriculum, and improving teacher performance through better preparation and proper incentives.[66] As the precise shape of the reforms is debated on particular campuses, it is vital that the voices of Christian humanists be joined with others of good will, on behalf of reform, which makes possible the education of the whole person. Trustees, administrators, and deans, as well as faculty members and students who serve on appropriate committees can promote policies that clearly place the well-being of students in the center of the academic enterprise. The opportunities are many and varied for members of the faith community to work with others in an effort to improve the quality of higher education so that a healthy personal development is facilitated. What is needed is the conviction that this is an essential aspect of bringing Christian witness to the campus.

---

66. We recall the four reports cited in footnote 8.

F. Developing Leaders for the Future

1. Potential Leaders on Campus

93. Campus ministry has the great opportunity to tap the immense pool of talent in our colleges and universities and to help form future leaders for society and the Church. Large numbers of intelligent and ambitious young people are on campuses, gaining the knowledge and skills needed to launch them into eventual positions of leadership in the world. Many of the older students at our colleges and universities are acquiring new knowledge and skills that will enhance their opportunities to influence their world for the good. The intense course of studies pursued by graduate students equips them with specialized knowledge that can be used for the common good. When international students, trained on our campuses, return to their own countries, they carry with them knowledge and skills that can be extremely valuable in promoting progress in their own societies. While not all of the students on campuses today will assume prominent leadership positions, everyone will have opportunities to provide some leadership in their various communities.

94. The large numbers of Catholics attending colleges and universities are potential leaders not only of society, but of the Church as well. Parishes require women and men who, in actively proclaiming the Gospel, combine commitment and good will with knowledge and skills. The Catholic community is in great need of more priests who will dedicate themselves to serving the needs of others. The religious orders are looking for new members who will live a life of dedicated service. In searching for this kind of church leadership for the future, we naturally turn to our colleges and universities, where so many of our talented young people are being educated.

95. The search for church leaders on campus should also extend to Catholic administrators and faculty. The local Church should make every effort to train individuals to carry out campus ministry on campuses where there are no professional campus ministry personnel. These men and women who are blessed with extensive education perform an important Christian service in the academic world and constitute an immense resource for church leadership. Not all of these individuals have the time or calling to assume leadership positions within the faith community. However, as a whole, they constitute a valuable pool of leadership talent that could be better utilized for the benefit of the Church.

2. Leadership in the Christian Perspective

96. From the perspective of faith, the Scriptures present a distinctive understanding of leadership. Jesus told his followers, "You are the light of the world . . . your light must shine before all so that they may see goodness in your acts and give praise to your heavenly father" (Mt 5:14-19). This suggests that all the disciples of Jesus carry the responsibility of offering personal witness in order to make a difference in the world and of using their influence to bring others to a greater appreciation of the goodness of God. This kind of leadership is to be carried out according to one's own unique talents. As the Apostle Paul indicated: "Just as each of us has one body with many members, and not all the members have the same function, so too we, though many, are one body in Christ and individually members one of another. We have gifts that differ according to the favor bestowed on each of us" (Rom 12:4-6). Paul also reminds us of the deep purpose involved in such gifts when he says, "To each person the manifestation of the Spirit is given for the common good" (1 Cor 12:7). In the Christian community, genuine leadership is based not on coercive power or high status, but on loving service that leads to the empowerment of others (Mk 10:42-45). Thus, the clear teaching of Scripture is that gifts and talents are not given simply for personal advantage; they are to be used generously for the benefit of others and for the good of society and the Church.

97. The Second Vatican Council recognized the great opportunities for this kind of Christian leadership and called on all adult Christians to prepare themselves for this task. "Indeed, everyone should painstakingly ready himself [or herself] personally for the apostolate, especially as an adult. For the advance of age brings with it better self-knowledge, thus enabling each person to evaluate more accurately the talents with which God has enriched [each] soul and to exercise more effectively those charismatic gifts which the Holy Spirit has bestowed on [all] for the good of [others]."[67] Thus, from the perspective of faith, it is clear that effective leadership in the contemporary world is connected both with a sense of loving service and with a more mature development in self-knowledge.

98. The nature of Christian leadership can also be understood from the viewpoint of the vocation we all receive from God. Through baptism, "all the faithful of Christ of whatever rank or status are called to the fullness of the Christian life and to the perfection of charity. By this holiness a more human way of life is promoted even

---

67. "Decree on the Laity," no. 30.

in this earthly society."[68] This baptismal vocation gives to every Christian the special task "to illumine and organize" temporal affairs of every sort "in such a way that they may start out, develop, and persist according to Christ's mind."[69] Individuals may choose to live out this general vocation as single persons, as members of the clergy or religious orders, or as married couples. In all of these states of life, there are opportunities large and small for exercising a leadership that is based on service and helps to humanize our world.

3. Strategies for Forming Christian Leaders

99. Campus ministers can facilitate the development of Christian leaders by encouraging members of the faith community to identify their gifts and to use them for the common good. Individuals must be helped to overcome their fears and to gain confidence in their abilities. They need proper training and opportunities to improve their leadership skills. For example, retreats for liturgical ministers can help them sense the importance of their roles at Mass and enable them to perform these roles prayerfully and competently. A leadership training session for officers in Catholic student organizations, at the beginning of the academic year, can give them added confidence and practical skills. Campus ministers who work with student organizers of a social justice project can provide them with Christian principles and practical advice that will enhance their effectiveness as current and future leaders.

100. In addition to developing leaders within the faith community, campus ministers should also encourage students to exercise their influence in other groups and activities. It helps to remind them that involvement in the life of their college or university is a significant factor in getting more out of the collegiate experience and that all Catholics on campus have the responsibility to work for the betterment of the academic community.

101. The development of leaders involves helping students to discern their vocations in life and to prepare for them. Most young people on campus today need guidance in preparing for marriage and family life. The preparation should include programs that encompass the following elements: the sacrament of marriage as an interpersonal relationship; the identity and mission of the family; the role of human sexuality and intimacy; conjugal love as union and as sharing in the creative power of God; responsible parenthood; and the couple's

---

68. "Dogmatic Constitution on the Church," no. 40.
69. Ibid., no. 9.

responsibilities to the larger community.[70] A significant number of collegians seriously consider vocations to the priesthood or religious life.[71] Campus ministers are in an excellent position to promote these vocations. A program in which campus ministers gather interested students together regularly for discussions and prayer is a valuable way of helping them discern the promptings of the Spirit. Students moving in the direction of the single life often need personal assistance in order to deal with societal pressures and cultural stereotypes.

102. In order to get more faculty members and administrators to exercise leadership in the faith community, campus ministers need to establish personal contact with them, offer them opportunities that fit their particular expertise, and provide them with training, if necessary. For example, counselors on campus could run marriage preparation and enrichment programs for the faith community, after studying the Church's teachings on marriage. It would also be helpful to gather the Catholic faculty and administrators together, on occasion, to give them a sense of group identity and to encourage their active participation in the Church on campus. This could be done through a retreat in which they explore ways of integrating their faith with their professional concerns. The more this integration takes place, the better role models they will be for students, who are the emerging leaders of society and the Church.

---

70. John Paul II, *On the Family,* no. 66.
71. Fee et al., *Young Catholics,* pp. 154-55.

Epilogue

103. In this pastoral letter, we have placed campus ministry in its historical and cultural context and have examined it from the viewpoint of the persons who carry it out, as well as the tasks they perform. We are convinced that this ministry is vitally important for the future of Church and society. As bishops, we recognize our responsibility to "see to it that at colleges and universities which are not Catholic there are Catholic residences and centers where priests, religious, and [lay persons] who have been judiciously chosen and trained can serve as on-campus sources of spiritual and intellectual assistance to young college people."[72]

104. The revised *Code of Canon Law* has reinforced this responsibility by reminding us that the diocesan bishop is to be zealous in his pastoral care of students, even by the creation of a special parish, or at least by appointing priests with a stable assignment to this care.[73] We know it is important to find dedicated persons for this ministry who have a solid faith, a love for the academic world, and the ability to relate well to both inquiring students and an educated faculty. They need proper training, which includes personal development, practical experience, and theological study. Advanced degrees are helpful in order to gain credibility in the academic world. We are committed to providing the best professional campus ministers possible and intend to hold them accountable for dedicated and creative service to the academic community. Our responsibilities extend to ensuring that within each diocese adequate funding is available for campus ministry and that there is an overall plan for allocating resources.

---

72. "Declaration on Christian Education," no. 10.
73. *Code of Canon Law*, (Washington, D.C.: Canon Law Society of America, 1983), nos. 813-814.

105. Our hope is that this pastoral letter will mark the beginning of a new phase in the history of Catholic campus ministry in the United States. In our vision of the new era, campus ministry will succeed more than ever before in forming the faithful into vibrant communities of faith and in empowering them to bring the light of the Gospel to the academic world. Campus ministry will be better understood and supported by the Church as a whole and will therefore be strengthened to make its voice heard in the center of campus life. The spiritual life of the Church on campus will be renewed so that it can be a more potent force, enabling the academic community to live up to its own ideals. The faith community will be more in touch with its Catholic roots so that it can confidently enter into deeper dialogue and more productive relationships with other religious groups on campus. A contemporary Christian humanism will flourish, which will demonstrate to all the value of an adult faith that has integrated the best insights of the culture. The Church on campus will be seen more clearly as a genuine servant community, dedicated to social justice, and therefore will be a more effective sign and instrument of the kingdom of peace and justice in the world. In the new era, the Church and higher education will find more productive ways of working together for the well-being of the whole human family. In our vision, campus ministry, empowered by the Spirit, faces a future bright with promise.